To James Leith
John's nephew, who was born on the day this
book was finished

FINEST OF THE FEW

The Story of Battle of Britain Fighter Pilot John Simpson

HECTOR BOLITHO

AMBERLEY

This edition first published 2013
First published in 1943 as *Combat Report: The Story of a Fighter Pilot*

Amberley Publishing
The Hill, Stroud
Gloucestershire, GL5 4EP

www.amberley-books.com

Copyright © The Alfred & Isabel & Marian
Reed Trust 1943, 2010, 2013

The right of Hector Bolitho to be identified
as the Author of this work has been
asserted in accordance with the Copyrights,
Designs and Patents Act 1988.
ISBN 978 1 4456 0705 4

British Library Cataloguing in Publication
Data.
A catalogue record for this book is
available from the British Library.

Typesetting and Origination by Amberley
Publishing.
Printed in the UK.

1

When I first met John in a ship coming home from Australia, he was twenty-one. As he walked up the gangway I saw that his legs and arms were covered with bandages. He told me afterwards that they hid the wounds of sixty-eight boils which had been lanced, without any anaesthetic, before he was put on to the stinking little schooner which brought him down the coast to Fremantle. His eyes were truthful and solemn; the eyes of a man guided by his sensibilities more than his mind. But he was quick to laugh. His face brightened at a joke and he obviously loved comfort and fun. These qualities went with the average human weaknesses and a rare talent for bringing out the best in everybody he met.

The bows of our ship were turned towards the Indian Ocean and the last albatross deserted us, to fly south again. We were moving towards the old world. John's melancholy adventure in Australia was over and he was coming home.

For five unhappy months he had been working as a jackaroo on a sheep station in the hungry stretches of the North-West. The men he worked with had been as hard as hell. They reeked of old filth, they lived with aborigine women, and they ate snakes, cooked on lids of biscuit tins. It was not a life for a boy who had grown up on the subdued fens of East Anglia.

John told me the story of his adventures in Australia one morning, as I sat on the side of the swimming bath. He had celebrated his twenty-first birthday on the way out from England. Two weeks after he found himself steaming past the sterile sand coast of West Australia, sharing a little ship with sheep and cattle.

'There were four of us in the cabin,' John told me. 'Four, and my cabin trunk. It was tied to my bunk with string. When the cyclone came, the trunk swayed and banged about. My companions were a shearer, with freckles as big and brown as pennies, a civil servant bound for Singapore, and a jackaroo.

'We went on slowly and came to the northern sweep of the coast. That's where you get pearls from the sea and wool from the land. I got to know the jackaroo and I learned a little of what was waiting for me, because my job was to be the same as his. We used to waste our time in the bar or hang over the rails, watching the ten-foot sharks cutting the water with their fins. He told me of all the taboos that would help me on my way. He said that I wasn't to know a sheep if I saw one. I wasn't to speak unless I was spoken to, and I was to be very humble and pretend that I had never ridden a horse in my life.'

John's ship steamed up the coast, past Onslow, which had been wrecked by a cyclone, and then to the port at which he was to land. It was in the far north. He went on shore, to the pub which was to be his home for thirteen days. 'There had been 25 inches of rain in three months,' he said. The usual fall was only 8 inches a year. 'So the landing ground was flooded and they told me I couldn't fly to the sheep station, fifty miles inland. The road was a succession of shimmering pools and creeks, so I couldn't drive. I just waited in that pub and watched my body slowly changing shape with the bumps where the mosquitoes and sandflies bit me. The people talked of nothing but cricket and drink and sex.'

2

I made John pause in telling his story. I had found an occupation for his idle days in the Indian Ocean. Diligently, with my suggestions but his own phrases, he wrote some 2,000 words on his adventure:

On the thirteenth day, the landing ground was clear of water and I was able to fly to the sheep station in an aircraft which they had been using over the northern wastes for twelve years. It was a closed machine and we were curled up inside, with our suitcases on our knees. We turned our faces towards the one window. It was cracked celluloid which let in a jet of sickly warm air onto our cheeks. For nearly an hour we flew over the barren country, leaving the sea behind us. At last we saw the river upon which the sheep station lay. We came to a cluster of gum trees and the aircraft descended on to the soft earth. We bumped towards a bedraggled contraption of a car. There were two men standing near. One was white and one was black. The white man was the storekeeper. (That man loved his store. The only relaxation he allowed himself was in the evening when he would curl himself up on his bed and play 'Wandering' on his banjo.)

We motored about a mile and crossed the river. We came to the plantation of gums and to the buildings, with the stretches of sand between them. The sand rose in little eddies. Sometimes, in the weeks after, that sand rose in fury and covered everything with a brown-red film. The homestead was clean enough. There was a maze of pens, a horseyard and a saddleroom. But there were no sheep. The eighty-thousand sheep were in the country beyond. There were a million-and-a-quarter acres of that miserable pasture upon which I was to work and ride and muster, in the months to come.

As I walked towards the building, the first time, one of the men offered me a cigarette. As I took it, he said, 'You know, it is not safe to take other people's cigarettes here. There is a good deal of venereal disease and as they all make their own cigarettes, it is rather risky to smoke them.' I was on the station hardly a week when one of the black women came to my room and suggested that we might do business. God, she was terrible. When I said no, she shrugged her shoulders and said, 'Well, will you lend me five shillings to play cards with?'

There were eight white men on the station. The manager was short, round and grey. He was severe. But he was kind at times. He always had a hell of a liver on Friday. I arrived on Friday, and it was the thirteenth.

One of the men had been a sailor. He had deserted twenty-six years before. He was old and thin and he talked a lot. He ate frogs and snakes and duck eggs, stale duck eggs, even when the baby ducks were already formed inside. The blacksmith was a little mad. He gave us tea in the blacksmith's shop every morning. The enamel mugs were so old that the holes in them were filled with rusty rivets. The talk during these morning teas was sheep and sex.

The builder was silent. He had been away from the station only twice in thirty years. There was a little Welshman who always wanted to lead me aside and talk of the old country. He still called it *Home*. The overseer was about thirty-six, a romancer and a leg-puller. Once when I was out mustering with him, our food was becoming short. He took a piece of bread and scattered dry curry powder on it. 'You know,' he said, 'it's almost as good as dipping your bread in your curry gravy.'

There was one out-camp man so sore with disease that he always wore pyjamas under his dirty clothes. There was a Chinese cook, round and short, with eyes that were always sore from the flies on his eyelids. There were about one hundred aborigines who were each paid ten shillings a week.

The loneliness was terrible. The men never used their watches because the sand choked them. When we were out camping, we lived by the sun and we ate when we were hungry. They seemed to be afraid of the world. They told me of the few times when they had been to Perth for a holiday. They said they had been lonely and anxious to be back on the station. They would not dare go in a lift. The most wonderful thing of all to them was the sliding staircase in a store in Perth. They had looked at it, but they had not dared to use it. And they had seen a Wurlitzer organ which rose from the orchestral well of a cinema theatre. They were drunk, I suppose. When they saw the floor moving and the organist rising with his manuals, they all thought they had d.t.'s and they rushed from the theatre.

Some of them did not even read the newspapers which arrived once each month by post. There were no books. One day I found myself reading the labels on the fruit tins, just to break away from the talk of sheep, sheep, sheep.

Sometimes at night we ate the white meat of a snake or the tail of a kangaroo. The meat of the kangaroo was sweet. The overseer called it *bonzer sweet meat*. He would throw the raw flesh on to the campfire. Snakes, lizards and bread were all cooked in the same way. When they were baked to a cinder, they were dragged out and scraped until you came to the juicy centre. The men had odd prejudices over food. They would not touch pork because pigs ate offal, and they wouldn't eat sausages because, they said, they were made from old, cheap bullocks.

A month passed before my cabin trunk and portable gramophone were brought from the port. The water from the floods had fallen very slowly. I had told the men about the gramophone and of my new records and they were very excited. I returned one day and they said, 'The gramophone has arrived, but it is very big and we cannot undo the locks.' They had attacked my wardrobe-trunk, thinking it was the gramophone. They did not like Tauber or Bing Crosby. Crosby's accent annoyed them. They liked the old tunes so I played them 'Wheezy Anna'. The songs they sang themselves were just noisy. There was one parody which they sang every night.

'When the moon shines bright on Charlie Chaplin
His boots are cracking
For want of blacking.
And his tiny trousers
They want mending
Before they send them
To the Dardanelles.'

One night I was lying in the shelter of the cart and the mosquito net, which was hung from posts in the ground. I smoked my last cigarette and watched the Southern Cross which was hanging in a deep blue sky. I was cool in my pyjamas. My companion never bothered to undress at night. I watched him crawl under his net and then I rolled eight cigarettes for the next day. This was my last job before going to sleep. I woke up as the stars were fading before the rising sun. When I moved on my hard bed, my body was sore. I sat up and found that my legs and arms were covered by ugly sores, like old boils. The overseer was still asleep. I was terrified. I remembered the warning about accepting cigarettes and I thought of the one the man had given me on the first day.

I crept over the ground and sat by the overseer until he was awake. I showed him my sores but he didn't seem to think much of them. 'A touch of Barcoo rot,' he said. 'Not enough vegetables. Mosquitoes and sudden change of climate.'

I lay on the ground all day. Next day I rode many miles with the sores rubbing against the saddle. For a week I went on with the mustering and at the end of the time I went back to the homestead with sixty-eight sores on my legs and arms. The flesh on my legs was rotting and I could pull it away with my fingers, like tender meat. From then on my memory is a bit dim. I travelled into the port hospital in a truck, fifty miles in four hours, over a terrible road. The truck had been full of sheep the day before and their smell attracted thousands of flies which settled on my sores and fed off them.

Then, I remember that I lay on a bed while the doctor and the nurse sat beside me, one cutting open the sores on the right side of my body and the other cutting open the ones on the left.

I stayed in the hospital four days and then I suddenly realised that nothing in the world would induce me to become a sheep farmer. When I was well enough, I went back over the fifty miles of road, packed my things and said, 'Goodbye.'

They were silent when they helped me to put my luggage on the car. I thought it was resentment until one of them walked a little way with me and said, 'You are right to go. If I had my time over again I wouldn't come here. It's living death, you know. That's what it is. It's no place for a boy like you. No place for a boy. It's living death.'

3

The Fen country may be black and cold and the people there may be a little crazy. But they are not lonely. It was unlikely that one of their sons would be able to sleep in that dry, empty country, night after night, without yearning for home.

It was John's body, not his spirit, that was broken. But he was obsessed with the idea that he had failed. One had to work very hard to shake him out of his gloom. On the night before we arrived in Colombo, we were leaning over the railings, smoking and talking. He told me the end of his story and then he said, 'You see, my trouble is that I have got an awful inferiority complex. That's my difficulty, and I don't know what I am going to do about it.'

One morning when we were near Aden, John told me of his days at school. He had played football and hockey, and his somersaults and hand springs had been the delight of all beholders. When I pressed him to talk of his education, he said, 'Oh, you mean things for my mind! Well, I hated Latin. There was geography and a bit of French. And I remember something about sodium in water and things like that. A Bunsen burner.'

What I really wished to find out was whether reading might help him, for he paced the deck hour by hour and seemed to have no relaxations. He told me that he had read very little at school. *The curfew tolls the knell of parting day. The something, something, something, twiddledy dee.*

What he lacked in knowledge of the reliable poets was more than made up for by his integrity. He was frank about his faults and lenient with the weakness of others.

Chapter Three

We came to Suez in the middle of June. The sun was so hot that the vultures seemed to sag with exhaustion as they wheeled in over the sand dunes. But above them, swift and serene, two silver aircraft flew towards the Sinai desert. We watched them for a long time until they were lost in the East. John turned to me then and said, 'You know, I think that I'd like to fly. I can remember when I was a boy in Ramsey. I was about four. It was in the last war. We lived near an aerodrome, and when the pilots were coming home they'd circle round the house, and if there was enough food my mother would spread a tablecloth on the tennis lawn to tell them that they could come to dinner. And one of them used to hold me over his head, with both hands, and run with me to give me the idea that I was flying.'

We went into the bar then and joined the deck-tennis players at their lime juices and sodas. As we went down to the dining saloon, John said again, 'You know, *that*'s what I'll do when I get back to England. I'll fly.'

4

John did not know the country through which we were passing. But I had been to Egypt, Palestine and Transjordan each winter for three years and I had come to know the pilots of the Royal Air Force who policed the desert. For some months in 1932, I had lived almost as an Arab, with the Amir Abdullah of Transjordan. Sometimes his brothers, King Ali and King Feisal, would come to stay. Then we would sit in the great tent at night, listening to a minstrel from Mekka, where Abdullah, Feisal and Ali had lived as boys. The palace was in the desert town of Amman, which was the Philadelphia of Roman days. There were Arab ponies for me to ride in the coolness of the late afternoon, and at night, sheiks and desert warriors would join us, to doze over their cups of bitter coffee or to throw their clattering dice on the backgammon board.

They were days of indolence for me. The Amir Abdullah's country was protected by the Royal Air Force. Marauding neighbours, bred upon pillage and rape, were easily subdued by the Fairey Gordons that flew over the lawless Arabs, dropping their salutary pamphlets. When this first literary appeal proved futile, machine guns were called upon to enforce the British argument.

As I lay in the garden of the palace during the long warm days, I saw the British aircraft flying over the desert where Abraham had walked; the same desert over which Lawrence led his Arabs, blowing up the Turkish railway lines on the way.

One day I left the Arab princes and travelled south to the Royal Air Force station at Ma'an. I lived for three months in a white, mud-walled fortress, which rose from the sea of burning sand like a stark and lonely ship. It was a strange life for me. My host was Pat Domvile, who was Intelligence Officer for the southern part of Transjordan. Pat had melted into the life of Arabia as naturally as Lawrence. He spoke perfect Arabic and the sheiks loved him. There were days of shooting buzzard and eating meals of sheep and rice; parties at the mess and, sometimes, alarming journeys in armoured cars which took me into the great dusty spaces of the desert. But our business was with the sky. We did not look along the road when people were coming to lunch with us. We looked up to the sun and the clouds.

Pilots would arrive from Baghdad and Damascus. Our letters were flown down to us from Jerusalem. Although we lived in the land where the ass and the camel meandered across the desert, as they did in the time of Jesus, we were completely air-minded.

To this day I know very little about flying. For me, all the mechanical arts are lost in a deep well of ignorance. So it was as men rather than pilots that the members of the Royal Air Force interested me. They seemed to be a new breed. They lived on laughter and justice, with a certain amount of poetry thrown in. They flew over Nazareth, with its slim cypresses against white walls; over the gaunt hills of Judea and the little houses of Bethany. Sometimes, when the Dead Sea was smooth as glass, they said they could look over the side of their aircraft and see the ruins of cities in the water below. It was not likely that they could fly over such romantic country without some of its poetry entering their souls.

I find it difficult to say why these pilots of ten years ago were different from other men. One fights shy of words like *sincere, just* and *kind*. Yet these are the words I should use. I think the chief attraction of the pilots lay in their lack of humbug, their ruthless contempt for pretence in others and their passionate belief in the Royal Air Force: not merely because it was a British institution. The flag-wagging days were over for them. The smooth voices of diplomacy, the slick arguments of Westminster and the 'by gad, old man' Englishman were packed away in dust and rosemary. Flying took these pilots into another world – a world of cloud and wind and rain. Their charter was in the sky and they were the companions of the sun. Naturally enough, they were cleansed of a good deal of the corruption and greed and artfulness which made the rest of us – anchored to the earth – seem to be rather unpleasant people. Their friendship was an exciting compliment. In them, I felt that England might find another chance.

Elizabethan sailors must have felt the same emotions as these pilots, in the great days of navigation. The Elizabethans found a new element – the sea – and they conquered it. They were great people. The pilots of the Royal Air Force had found a new element in the air, and they were conquering it. One felt that they also were to become great.

The pilots and airmen lived on faith in each other and this seemed to segregate them from other men. One morning a crippled aircraft arrived from Egypt. The pilot lunched with us while his machine was being repaired. I can remember saying to him, 'It is wonderful that you can have such faith in your mechanics.' He said, 'Oh, yes. That *is* the wonderful thing about the Service. One just knows that the ground staff will never let you down.'

He flew off to Egypt again, and in the afternoon I walked up to the hangars and found the sergeant who had been in charge of the repairs. I told him what the pilot had said. He answered, 'Oh, the boot is on the other foot. Imagine what it feels like when you are a craftsman, to have your work completely trusted like that … to know that the pilots place their lives in your hands.'

It was upon such faith that the Air Force was being built.

5

As John and I came near to Suez, I sent a wireless to some of the pilots who had since been posted from Transjordan to Ismailia. It is sad for me to look back on the list of friends I made during those winters because few of them are still alive. Rodney Wilkinson, who was with Sir Wilfred Freeman in Jerusalem, was killed in the summer of 1940. George Mooreby, the dearest and most generous scapegoat who ever had an overdraft, crashed into Southampton Water. Kenneth Ferguson, who once flew me over the Dead Sea: who used to walk with me through the dusty streets of Amman, was lost early in the war. And Philip Hunter, who once flew me upside down and inside out at Cranwell, was lost while leading his squadron, soon after Dunkirk. It is all a page of dead faces: of the loneliness which is one of the chief punishments of war.

The swastika was merely a faint shape on the horizon in the summer of 1934 when John and I steamed towards Suez. The ship glided into the Canal and towards Ismailia. In those days I travelled grandly and I always fostered any little signs of pomp. The Suez Canal Company sent out a fine launch to take us ashore so that we might make merry while the ship glided on towards Port Said. Philip Hunter was waiting for us and, for the first time in his life, John ate breakfast in a Royal Air Force mess. I saw him wake up in an instant. Those who watch the Service at a distance, without knowing the careless nonsense, the loyalties that are bred, the thrill of living at double speed: the dazzling fun and the deep-rooted theme of truth and affection that binds all these things together, have missed the gayest and yet the saddest world: a complete world within itself. For the Air Force draws you into its secrets and fills your life, even if you live on its edge as I have done, wearing no wings. It was to be all of John's life. I was there to see the beginning of it, on that summer morning, eight years ago.

6

The war has helped civilians to appreciate the bravery and achievements of the aircrews in the Royal Air Force. But I doubt if they will ever comprehend the spirit which binds the Service together. The pilots, navigators, gunners and ground crew speak, laugh and think in their own secret tongue. They are satisfied with this secrecy and are shy and even suspicious of any attempt to intrude upon it. Their jokes are their own and their pleasures – simply as the games which children play – are halved when they have to be shared with strangers. This character isolates a Service mess from civilian life and it is not easy to define.

Before the war, members of the Royal Air Force were not popular among prim and conventional people. They drove noisy cars into ditches. Because their lives were uncertain and because money was therefore a means to an end and not a possession to be coveted, some of them were casual about worldly affairs. Their links with life outside the Service were transient and unimportant.

I saw all these things in the Service when I first met the pilots ten years ago. I saw John assume this knowledge and this character as he grew older. I saw him touch the fringe of it on that July morning, when we drank and dozed and laughed on the banks of the Suez Canal.

7

We lived through eight very silly hours ashore while the ship was slithering through the Canal to pick us up at the other end. The Suez Canal Company gave me a car so that John and I could wander in Ismailia, and along the banks, up to the last moment when we were supposed to climb back on to our ship at Port Said. Philip Hunter knew that we were coming and he had flown over the *Malaya,* diving in sweeps of welcome, perilously near the masts.

The pilots did their flying early in the morning in the East – before breakfast. They were already relaxing when we arrived at the mess at Ismailia: clustering about their English meal. Bacon and eggs! Incongruous food to find, with palm trees, sunbaked sand and the elongated lines of the Egyptian landscape beyond the windows.

I don't remember very much of what happened afterwards. I think there were about six pilots with us. We tumbled into the dignified motor car, pell-mell as whitebait on a plate, and sped along the edge of the canal to Port Said. John sat next to Philip Hunter, a grand type of pilot who had the essence of the Royal Air Force in his blood. The Service was still small and those already in it cared very much about the quality of the fledglings who wished to fly. Philip took trouble to talk to John, at the moment when his enthusiasm was young and warm. When we arrived in Port Said, they still went on talking shop. Master and pupil were well met.

Some years afterwards, Philip Hunter told me that he had felt that John would be a good pilot. 'I encouraged him to join' is all that he said. There was already a patient fatherliness in the pilots. They wished to hand on the secret of their happiness to those who deserved to share it.

Some ridiculous incidents survive from that day in the Egyptian sun! We found a hotel in Port Said. In the main hall was a pretentious balcony. While we were there, a child dropped its teddy bear over the railing, into the hall below. We all tried to throw the teddy bear back again – a formidable height for such a light toy. I remember how young I felt when I alone succeeded, only because, as I threw it up, I closed my eyes and willed the strength into my hand.

Philip Hunter and the others stayed with us until it was time to look for the ornamental boat which was to take us off to the ship. But we swayed a little from hospitality, and I did not dare take my tipsy friends to the sedate little craft, with its gilt ornaments and its straight-backed crew. So we gave it the slip and we hired a stinking little Egyptian rowing boat, with a still more stinking little Egyptian to man it, and we crept to the other side of the ship, away from the fashionable parade, a little abashed by the sudden glare of the sun and the responsibility of climbing up a gangway.

I remember that the pilots all liked John and that they exchanged addresses with him as the whistle blew and the stewards cried, 'All ashore.' I remember also that as we steamed out of Port Said into the broad spaces of the Mediterranean, John said to me, 'Now those are the sort of chaps I understand.' Then he harped upon the sad theme of his inferiority complex, which might have been tiresome if he had not been so sincere and so eager to break his way into freedom.

8

The first weeks after his return from Australia were fretful and undecided for John. He did not settle into his old habits with any ease. It was amusing for me to see him emerge as a smart little Londoner, with bowler hat and gloves and umbrella. There was a certain clean correctness about his clothes which was a key to his inner scrupulousness. But he was not at home in the Berkeley and the Ritz. He pretended to enjoy it all, but I think that his heart was in the country.

Chapter Eight

About this time I began my biography of James MacKay, the 1st Lord Inchcape. I was faced by a mountain of papers so formidable that my heart was cold when I saw the filing cabinets in Lady Inchcape's London house. They provided the momentary anchor which John needed. He joined me in sorting them and, helped by his extraordinary tidiness of mind, he became a good librarian.

The background against which he lived is important. His mother, a lovely, intelligent woman, shared life with him in a degree uncommon in a parent. To see them doing a crossword puzzle together was a delight. They would pause to exchange memories of the farm in Huntingdonshire; memories of which they were not in the least shy. They laughed easily together. They shared one memory which is important to this story. John's mother remembered the Air Force in the last war. Her house had been open to the pilots. With an instinct which had survived the years, she remembered their unique character and their gaiety of mind. Little stories of them crept into the conversation and perhaps they kept the seed which had been sown in Ismailia alive in John's mind. His three sisters were equally beautiful and he adored them. He had neither father nor brother to compete in these affections.

I bought a house in Essex when I returned to England, and John and I decided to share it until he made plans for the future. We made a garden and we collected furniture. His mother stayed with us and supervised my clumsy experiments at furnishing a kitchen. She cooked us our first real meal, with only a servant from the village to come for an hour or so – so that our fun at housekeeping should not be disturbed. This was in the perfect September of 1934. John took off his correct bowler hat and he put away his folded umbrella. We set about making vegetable and flowerbeds from the neglected farmyard. My fingers were all thumbs at first, for I was a seed catalogue gardener and not much use at anything. I resigned myself to John's guidance. He seemed contented when he was digging and planting. There was a moaning old barn in which we spread the plants as they arrived. In later years we had to move almost every tree we had planted. But the joy of that first summer was incomparable. I made my first home in England and I spread myself into the luxuries of a little lord of the manor. We dug and planted and ate, and in the evening we were able to sleep from simple physical exhaustion.

But winter came. The melancholy winds of East Anglia blew in from the North Sea. I saw then that John stirred with his old restlessness. The occupations of summer came to an end and there was little to do in the garden. Sometimes, in the evening, he would suddenly take out his car and drive off to one of the little pubs that were scattered about the country. He did not seem able to settle into a chair beside the fire and read a book.

One evening Batchy Atcherley (now Group Captain R. L. R. Atcherley, OBE, AFC) flew down in his little Avro Avian monoplane to stay with us. It was our first link with flying since our return to England: the first tangible reminder of John's promise. That evening, beside the fire, we talked away many hours and I saw John's intention becoming clear again.

9

The story must go back for a moment to my first winter in Transjordan when I was living with the Amir. The most startling pilot on the Air Force Station, which was 3 miles away from the palace, was Richard Atcherley, whose fierce vitality and original spirit were all wrapped up in the nickname of 'Batchy.' He was tall and lean and so energetic that he always seemed to be walking one pace ahead of himself. He brought such originality, eagerness and wit to bear on everything he did that one already saw the promise of scrambled eggs on his cap. He kept a lion cub as his pet, until it grew quarrelsome and hungry. Then it was taken to a zoo in Egypt, where he visited it every year, until one sad day when it no longer remembered him.

A good deal of my pleasure during those months in the desert came from Batchy's friendship. We acted together in a touching production of 'Journey's End'. Leonard Cockey (now Air Commodore L. H. Cockey), with the happiest gurgle of a laugh I have ever heard, was The Colonel. Lloyd-Williams (now Captain J. J. Lloyd Williams, MC, Chief Constable of Aberystwyth) was Osborne. Batchy was Stanhope, Eric Loverseed was Raleigh, and I was Hardy. I had to sing 'One and two, it's with Maud and Lou' as the play opened.

There were guest nights after which Batchy would lead us into almost criminal escapades. Tar barrels were hurled down the hills. The notes from the mess piano were torn out, one by one, and Batchy would fling them into the valley. There was a conscientious little Met Officer who would spend the next day hunting for the missing notes all down the slope. It was amusing to see him searching for F sharp or A flat among the stubble. He would put them all back into the piano again with meticulous care, only to whet Batchy's appetite for next guest night. Once, they tried to abscond in the Amir's train which was getting up steam at the station in the valley. Nobody could work it, so they took a jigger instead and sped along the railroad track towards Zerka, where the Transjordan Frontier Force were stationed.

When the railway lines ended, they just forced the jigger over the sand until it arrived at the door of the mess. Batchy was the ringleader of it all. But behind his façade of practical jokes and attractive foolishness was an austerity of character which compelled one's faith.

With all his nonsense, Batchy was a brilliant pilot. One night, we were sitting before the mess, with a soft wind blowing the fine sand of the desert over us. Batchy whispered in my ear, 'I think I'll fly up and take a look at Jerusalem.' I went with him.

It was the most amazing flight of my life – not only for the beauty of what we saw but because Batchy could give his passenger the sensation of flight with peculiar genius. We flew in a Fairey Gordon, our faces free to the wind that blew over the desert. There was a vast moon over Jerusalem. We flew up towards it, so that we could look down and see the road that ran into the city from Bethany. Then out to the edge of the Mediterranean, where we could see the final edge of silver water moving restlessly against the coast. Then we flew towards Mount Hermon, with its summit hidden under snow. I covered that great span of country in what seemed to be a handful of minutes and I was back in front of the mess in time to drink my iced whisky and soda before we all went to bed.

I think that Batchy had given me my first smell of the romance of flight. But he had done more than that. One Sunday, we had taken sandwiches and bottles and driven out to the desert. We found an oasis, with a few gallant oleanders defying the arid stretches of sand. There we had sprawled and talked. I saw in him all the latent courage of the Royal Air Force. His own mind and passion made me believe in the Service more than ever. I like to think that I was sensitive enough to comprehend the tide of his faith. He was jealous of the integrity of the Service and proud of its adolescent vigour. It was impossible not to share his belief – that there was already a spirit within the Service which would help to save Britain if she ever came upon an hour of need.

10

My neighbour in Essex was Norman Myhill, a farmer who had made the first gestures of friendship when we arrived with our vanload of furniture. He had walked across the fields to greet me, with vegetables, eggs and milk. I can best describe him as kindness itself. The Myhills had farmed in the county for hundreds of years and Norman grew out of the earth of Essex as naturally as its crops and trees. Batchy was to land his aircraft in one of Norman Myhill's stubble fields. We had lighted a fire – scavenging in the ditches for dry sticks and pulling up damp grass roots – so that there would be a thread of smoke to guide Batchy after he had passed the stunted tower of Hempstead church.

It was still exciting in those days for a guest to arrive by air. So we stood in the field, Norman, John and myself, searching the sky.

The boys from the village ran up the lane in young delight when the aircraft landed in the stubble. Batchy brought the aircraft to rest within the shelter of the hedge and we made our way to the house, after fortifying ourselves for the walk with some of Norman's sloe gin.

John is a bit pompous about shaking cocktails. He likes to think he can perform miracles beyond the capacity of clumsy hands like mine, I had come to know the phrase, 'Would you like one of *my* dry martinis?' very well. So we drank and ate and, as the night closed in, we sat before the fire and talked. The sitting room was already comfortable, in a calm and shabby fashion. I think that I can say that I had created a room which invited you to flop into a chair and relax.

Batchy and I talked of Transjordan and Palestine; of the friends we had shared and of flights we had made. He was at his best. Long after, John recalled the evening to me in a letter:

> I was silently thrilled and I prayed that some day I might be able to do the same myself. I listened to the stories that you and Batchy told, of Ismailia and the Near East. And your stories of playing backgammon with the sheiks, and Batchy talking of the clouds over the desert, and the bumps. And his shooting up a garden party. I drank it all in and made up my mind, while you were both sitting in front of the fire, to go up to the Air Ministry and join the day after.

Next morning we went over to Norman Myhill's field to say 'Goodbye' to Batchy. There was a mark on one wing where a horse had bit it some weeks before. I remember that Batchy's aircraft was so tiny that he could not taxi it over the rough earth of the field; he had to leave the engine ticking over while he steered the machine by walking beside it and holding the wing, much as he might have guided a bicycle by the handlebars. When he had taken off we walked home again.

John went to London. He came back on the evening train with a Form 2110 from the Air Ministry. It was his application for a commission in the Royal Air Force. I really think that he was already a changed man. A sudden definiteness came into his actions. It was as if a lot of the straggling ends of his thought had suddenly been tied together.

I was sitting in the library of the Athenæum on the day that John received news of his acceptance for the Service. I remember him hurrying into the room, eager as a youngster, holding the foolscap envelope in his hand. He never did say much on such occasions, but his face told its tale. The day is sharp in my memory because of a pleasant but sad coincidence. At the table next to us were Lord Sempill and Kingsford Smith, drinking their coffee. It was the day before Kingsford Smith's last flight from England, on the journey which ended with his being lost in a mangrove swamp off the coast of Tenasserim.

John whispered: 'That's Kingsford Smith,' and at that moment, Lord Sempill leaned over to me and said: 'Have you got a Virginian cigarette for Kingsford Smith? Mine are all Turkish.' John jumped to his feet and opened his cigarette case. I whispered the news to Kingsford Smith and he played up like a lamb. It was rather pleasant that he should be the first person to congratulate him.

John was obviously delighted. He leapt down the stairs of the Athenæum two at once, to the distress of an old member who was ascending at the same time.

11

Three months were to pass before John began his training. With typical extravagance he drew 200 pounds from the bank and bought a ticket for New York. 'I've seen Africa and Australia. I'd like to see America,' he said. It was like him to buy a second-class ticket and change to first when he was no more than an hour out of Southampton. He wrote from the ship:

My cabin was so depressing. I had to share it with a horrible little man. He was sick the moment we left Southampton and he threw all his cigarette-ends into the basin. Everything depressed me so much that I went the whole hog and transferred to 1st. I can now talk with fairly sensible people and eat and sleep in comfort. It would have spoiled all my trip if I had stayed in the blunt end. I play ping-pong all day, as it's the only exercise I can get. It's extraordinary how quickly one gets good at it.

He wrote me one more letter, from the aircraft in which he flew back from Chicago to New York:

The aircraft is very quiet and comfortable. I may smoke and drink and eat and even sleep. We arrived at Cleveland ten minutes ago to refill the petrol tanks. Our next stop is New York, I hope. How terrible about Kingsford Smith! I see that he is missing. You will remember that I said that I felt it would happen this time. He has done so many risky flights. But it is very sad. Having met him makes it all the more so.

There is a beautiful sunset. I am way up 12,000 feet above the clouds. Only occasionally can I see a twinkling light on the ground or a silver river. The sun has disappeared quickly and only an orange-blue streak remains out of the blackness. We are doing 200 miles an hour. Think of it! Chicago-New York in three-and-a-half hours!

I have been standing beside the pilot. He won't let me play with the controls. It all seems so simple and 'George' seems to be doing all the work. The instruments are astounding. One needs a dozen eyes. How awful, the responsibility of these two men with their cargo of millionaires and important mails! We are still flying above the clouds. They look like a mass of cotton wool. It seems incredible that the little *pip pip* in his ears, which I can hear every now and then, is able to tell him where he is. I asked him, 'May I try and fly,' and he muttered something about the Federal Law. I told him that I would be in the Air Force in two months' time and that I hoped I would be flying something smaller and more personal than this big Lockheed. I told him that I hoped to be in fighters.

12

The *Europa* was delayed by fog on her way from New York. Halfway across the Atlantic, John won twenty pounds in the ship's sweepstake, so he spent some of it by telephoning me, to confirm the date when his flying instruction was to begin. He was anxious, he said, in case the fog kept him late.

I don't remember much of what happened following his arrival back in England. We spent a few days at Windsor, and on Christmas Day we went to the service in St George's Chapel. The war has made it all seem so long ago. (Four weeks later, I was to stand in St George's once more, to see the coffin of King George V being lowered into the vault.)

John went from Windsor to his civil flying school at Ansty, four miles or so from Coventry. I might as well allow his own letters to tell the next part of the story. He wrote to me from *The Limes,* on 5 January:

The house where I am billeted is called *The Limes*. I think that describes it, don't you? The house is red brick, with a tiled roof and a circle of grass in front. It's just like any other house. The woman is a bit fierce. Wizened and thin and bitter looking. Her husband was sitting at the bottom of the stairs in a chair. He seems to live in it. He is thinner still. He looks as if he'll die at any moment. It's a bit depressing. He's got a hole in his chest and a sort of tube through which he breathes. He can speak through his mouth, but his chest makes such a noise that you can't hear what he says. When I went into the living room, there were about eight other pupils there, the chief instructor and the CO of the station at Ansty.

That's where we are to be taught to fly. We are the first course. The CO is called Poppy Pope (now Wing Commander R. P. P. Pope, DFC, AFC). He is a charmer. He's a civilian, of course. They all are. He taught Bernard (Bernard Rubin, John's brother-in-law. After twenty-five hours' solo flying, he did a five hour blind flying course with Pope at Hamble and then flew to Australia and back, alone, in a Leopard Moth. Bernard Rubin died in 1936) to night fly before he flew out to Australia. I met the others. The nicest of them is Dennis Collins (Dennis Collins was killed at Kenley in 1938 while teaching somebody to fly by night). He was an artist in Chelsea. He seems a bit young to fly. He's got a baby face and hasn't had to shave yet. There's another chap I like, Jack Sullivan (Jack Sullivan was killed at the beginning of the war, in France). He's a Canadian from Montreal. He has already flown solo in Canada. He has a nice face. There are two other Canadians as well, Manly Gaunce (Manly Gaunce was killed while leading his squadron into battle in the late summer of 1941) and Charlie Olsson. I feel a bit of a fool because they have flown solo as well. I share a room with them. It's got a sort of rose and ivy leaf pattern on the wallpaper. The Canadians have a guitar. They sat on the side of their beds and played and sang 'Coming Down the Mountain' before they turned in for the night. We don't go to the aerodrome until tomorrow. I can't write any more now. The others have turned in. The old woman came up and said we had to stop the guitar and the singing. Gaunce called her a bloody old buzzard. I think she will need watching.

Two days later, he wrote again:

Life has been very hectic. I've been too tired at night to write. On the first day we went eight miles to the aerodrome. There was a bit of a muddle there, as the aerodrome is only partly built. They have joined a number of fields together to make the landing ground and some of the old hedges and fences are still there. It makes landing a bit dangerous. Some parts are bare, reddish soil. There is one hangar, a clubhouse and one classroom. Everything else is being built. Dennis Collins is in the same class as I am. And Sullivan. I am pleased because I like them most. Collins draws nude women for us and he has given us some for the walls of our room. They all have upturned breasts and legs coyly posed so that they just manage to cover what matters most. Sullivan and I have become good friends. I like him more and more.

I hope you'll be pleased. On the first day, Poppy Pope came and said one of us must be senior pupil. He chose me. I suppose it is because I am so old. Anyway, I am pleased. Sullivan has to assist me. On the first day we had to sign hundreds of papers. Then we were given flying suits, helmets, gloves and parachutes. And we had to sign papers about pay and next of kin and all that. Our instructor is Sergeant Tribe. We liked each other from the start. He is a great, big, fat, oldish man. Very fit. He says that he will take me up tomorrow. We are to train on Avro Cadets.

The bloody old buzzard will be the death of us. She snaps at her poor old husband. I am sorry for him. He sits there wheezing in the hall and she doesn't seem to have any sympathy for him. The food is usually our old friends, tomato soup, meat and two vegs. She is mean with the food and she grumbles if we take too much butter. She grumbles if there is hair oil on the pillows and cigarette ash on the carpet. It's like being back at school. Last night she grumbled because we put too much coal on the fire. When she went out we had our revenge. We just emptied the coal scuttle and made a hell of a blaze. I'll write after my flight tomorrow.

On 11 January, John made his first flight with Sergeant Tribe. He wrote to me that evening:

When Sergeant Tribe arrived I was already standing by the cockpit, playing with the controls. I had my flying suit on, ready. I moved the stick to one side and said, 'That's the way you turn it, isn't it?' He smiled and was very nice about it. But I had boobed. He said, 'Not quite, but you'll learn soon enough.'

It's a dual control machine of course. I sat in the back cockpit and Sergeant Tribe was in front of me. I must say I was a bit frightened. It all seemed so complicated. He told me over the earphones what everything did. He was very patient and calm with me because they must get a bit browned off with pupils, learning all the time. We were in the air for half an hour. I did not look out much. I kept my eyes in the cockpit. It came to me slowly what all the instruments and movements meant. Then he asked me if I'd like to try and fly it. I was a bit scared when he said, 'OK, you've got her.' The nose began to drop and I didn't like it much. It seemed as if we must just hit the ground. I'd let the stick go forward. He waited to see if I'd do the right thing and pull it back. But I didn't and I could feel it being pulled as he took over. The nose came up again on to the horizon. Sergeant Tribe said, 'OK that's enough now. We'll be doing some more. I must go back and take up some of the other pupils.'

I think the Avro Cadet is the nicest aeroplane in the world, but I suppose that's because I've never flown anything else. Sullivan flew today for the first time, but Dennis Collins has to wait until tomorrow. Of course Sullivan did well. I think I told you before that he has flown in Canada. He tells me that he was a mounted policeman. He knows more about life than I do. He knows all the good nightclubs. The others don't. I really have to do a job as senior pupil. I had to stop Gaunce and Olsson kicking a football through the classroom window which they do, with the utmost regularity. I just have to stop them breaking things and pinching the ink. I like Poppy Pope more and more. He's a bit fierce, but kind as a lamb. He's a wonderful organizer and an expert on night flying. We are not allowed to drink with the instructors. I think this is a pity as we would get to know them so much better.

The bloody old buzzard hates music. We can't play the guitar or sing. And the poor old wheezing husband is not allowed to turn on the wireless. He does, but she turns it off. It's pretty hard as he can do nothing but sit. I've met a South African, Jack Roulston. He's tough as hell. Before he came here he worked in a gold mine on the Rand. He is the same age as myself. We are the oldest on the course. I am not good at the lectures. Theory of Flight and Armament are the worst. I don't seem able to concentrate.

13

At the end of January, John wrote to me again. He had just been listening to the broadcast of King George's funeral service at Windsor.

I heard the service. He was a good man, wasn't he? The ground is covered with snow. But what I want to tell you about is my first solo last Friday. I flew dual for eight hours and then I had my test for solo with the chief flying instructor. Three spins each way and three landings and take offs. That all went very well, and when I came down all the pupils and the instructor were waiting for me, to see my first solo ... the first solo anyone has flown from Ansty.

I had one cigarette and then I climbed into the machine, very confident and very pleased. As I taxied out to get into wind, I could hear faint cries of good luck. I sat still for a minute and then away. Round the aerodrome I flew, very happy. Twice round and then down to the small field where everyone was waiting for me. I didn't look at them and made a really good landing, taxying up to where they stood. I stopped the machine and got out. Everyone was charming and apparently I had done my first job well.

No one else has gone solo yet. So I am well ahead of everyone.

I am sorry about Bisto. She must have been indiscreet during those two days. I do hope it was a nice dog and not that dreadful greyhound.

A few days later the course had to move to Eastleigh, near Southampton, because Ansty was flooded. John wrote again:

Chapter Thirteen

There was great excitement the other day at Eastleigh when we heard that a new aeroplane called the Spitfire was going to do a test flight. It is apparently the land version of the Supermarine floatplane which, you will remember, won the Schneider trophy. I had just landed after some blind flying with Poppy Pope when it taxied out. It has an enormous wooden propeller and is silver and looked highly polished. But it is very small. We were not allowed to go near. It is very secret. It took off in a strange way because it didn't point into wind as we always do, but thirty-five degrees across it and then straightened into wind when the throttle was opened. Sergeant Tribe told me that this was because of the terrific torque on the airscrew. It raced across the aerodrome. I felt rather sorry and sick for the people who have to test out new aeroplanes. But it got off the ground very quickly and it was a great thrill seeing the undercarriage disappear. I have never seen a fighter with a retractable undercarriage before. There were little puffs of black smoke as it climbed at an incredible angle into the sky. It was lost from view in a few minutes.

I then went up with Sergeant Tribe to do some aerobatics.

14

Early in May of 1936 John hired his first private aircraft and landed in the field beside the house. It was a great day. Norman and I had worked all the afternoon of the day before, gathering dead branches to build a bonfire which was 8 feet high before we finished it. We added a little petrol and welcomed John with a column of flame and smoke so fierce that the surrounding cowslips fainted from the heat. There was a scar in the field all through the summer. John brought his sister Ruth, in a Hornet Moth, and landed like a bird. He stepped out of the aircraft and shook my hand with so much authority that I was almost shy. His hesitancy had gone and I was abashed by the definite way in which he talked. He chaffed me for my little bits of pomposity, which he had always accepted without demur.

He no longer needed a guiding mind. When he took off again in the late afternoon, I walked back to the house with a pleasant sensation of pride. One more pilot had found himself in the character of the Royal Air Force. All the reluctance and diffidence of five months before were forgotten. John's inferiority complex, which he never mentioned again, had faded away.

We didn't talk much of war in those days. But the Air Force was slowly capturing the countryside and, five or six miles from my house, a pleasant old farm was turned into an aerodrome. We were soon shaken out of our rural peace. I had bought my farm and my house to escape from the hurly burly and to rest a little. But my rest became a myth. Some of the pilots from Debden were John's friends and they took possession of my house almost as soon as they arrived.

Gigantic hangars rose from the placid fields. A long weather-boarded hut was built for the officers' mess, and the village girls walked out of a Sunday evening on the arms of the boys in blue. Noisy cars roared down our peaceful lanes and I was dragged from my remote little house and made the first honorary member of the mess. Some of the old ladies in their gardens did not welcome the change. They sat beneath their cedar trees and rattled their tea cups in protest as the aircraft swept low over their houses. They wrote to *The Times* and to the Member of Parliament because beauty was being chased out of England by the hell birds that screamed overhead, day and night.

But they were happy days. The Station Commander was Poppy Pope (almost every pilot named Pope in the Air Force is given the nickname of Poppy. Poppy Pope, who commanded Debden, is now Group Captain P. R. Pope), who stood 6 feet 2 in his socks and who imprisoned the spirit of an imp in his gigantic frame. Every Sunday morning I threw a party. When I felt rich, we drank champagne. When I was poor, we drank beer. The house was always wide open. They came, Dickie Lee who was to win his DSO and DFC before he was lost in August of 1940; Laurie Lorimer, who was also to do well in battle, before he was killed in May of 1940; Bill Sykes who is now flying with the Fleet Air Arm; Rhys-Jones; George Feeny who was posted missing while serving with the Fleet Air Arm, in June of 1940; Eric Stapleton, now serving with the RAF in Rhodesia; dear old Boothby with his oily car. And Jeff. We called him Social Type Jeff because he was something of a gallant, with the smartest blue suit on the Station. He was also to be killed in action, in August of 1940.

But those were the careless days of peace.

The pilots came to rest in the house when they were tired from flying and they brought their gramophone records to play on my radiogramophone. When they came in a party, they would be noisy and gay. When they came alone, they would be quiet, and eager to talk before the fire. For there was never a bore among them. They never read any of my books and I never talked to them of my work. Their life was mine. Sometimes, we would have somebody beautiful, like Dorothy Dickson, for them to meet. They adored her.

The servants also fell under the spell of the pilots, who never bothered to tell *me* when they were hungry. Mitzi would cook sausages for them, or they would cook them themselves. They would help her wash the dishes and make their own beds if they wished to stay all night. This tide of young energy changed my life. The pilots came to me with their troubles: an angry bank manager, an impatient tailor, or even the indignant mother of a favourite blonde had to be pacified. I wrote their letters for them and I even interviewed their bank managers when I thought they were going a little too far with their demanding letters. The pilots would fly over the house and drop an evening newspaper for me because I could not have them delivered from the village. We scoured the countryside for pretty girls for them on Sunday mornings. Norman, the gardener, became their friend and their slave.

When John came home on leave the house was like a small Air Force mess. I think he enjoyed it because pilots are a clanny lot and they like the exciting round of their own shop.

John wrote to me from Sealand, a little time before this:

Last night we had boxing and I drew someone a stone heavier than myself. I had hell for one minute. Then he knocked me out. Today I have two black eyes and a broken nose. But I can take it. Empire air day was a great success. Ten thousand people. I did some formation flying and some aerobatics to thrill the crowds.

He had something to talk about when he came home on leave. I looked on and smiled, with the sensations of a father whose hopes have come true.

For some years before I bought my house in Essex, I lived in the shadow of Windsor Castle, writing the biography of Queen

Victoria. Apparently I had remained adaptable, for when I had a couple of hundred pounds to spare I ran my electric wires underground so that my field would make a perfect landing ground. I subscribed to *The Aeroplane* and gave up *Country Life*. I instinctively peppered my vocabulary with the pilots' slang and I left the old ladies under the cedar trees severely alone. We no longer spoke the same language.

Sometimes John's mother stayed with me when he came on leave with his friends. We had no place in the conversation. We just sat before the fire, listening to the confused enthusiasms of another generation, and occasionally looking at each other in amused recognition of the fact that we were being allowed to listen on the fringe of another world.

15

The victories of the Royal Air Force startled Britain soon after the present war began. The numbers of the squadrons were kept out of the newspapers, but people in country towns began to talk of those stationed on nearby aerodromes with local pride, as if they were their own regiments. Few seemed to realise that some of them were old and already rich in history, with trophies on their walls recalling the victories of a quarter of a century before.

The newspapers began to sing the praises of the pilots of 43 Squadron, although they were not then allowed to mention the Squadron's number. 43 brought down their first enemy aircraft in the war, over England in January of 1940. We were all concerned with the battle in hand, and there was no time to remember that 43 had been formed in 1916 (43 Squadron was formed at Stirling in 1916, by Major Sholto Douglas, now Air Chief Marshal Sir Sholto Douglas, C-in-C, Fighter Command) and that it was rather a veteran. While the outside world discovered the Squadron as something new and exciting, there were many older pilots within the Service who saw in the valour of the young merely a new chapter added to an old story. Captain Balfour, the Under Secretary of State for Air, had flown with 43 in 1917. He watched its new life with fatherly interest, sometimes escaping from his desk at Whitehall to fly with the new aircraft that were so different from the machines he had used in France, twenty-five years before.

When John joined 43, in October 1936, the Squadron was stationed at Tangmere, 4 miles from Chichester. In other parts of England, most of the Air Force stations were new. But Tangmere already had a small tradition. Its buildings were mature and its trees had settled into the earth. No. 1 Squadron and No. 43 Squadron had been there since 1926, each with its souvenirs of the last war. On guest nights the mess table shone with good silver. 43 held the trophy for gunnery and the Sassoon trophy for the annual pin-pointing competition. It was a silver bowl which held three bottles of champagne. On the walls of the mess were the propeller of a Hun shot down by No. 1 Squadron during the last war and the Squadron memorial of 43 – an enemy propeller with the names of past heroes beneath it.

There was a spirit at Tangmere for John to take unto himself, according to his talents and his sense of history.

John had one unpardonable fault – which survives to this day. He seldom dated his letters. So I can only print the following passages from them and explain that they were written between December of 1936 and June of 1937:

December

Much has happened in the last few days. Last night we had a guest night, and Jack Sullivan and I had to buy champagne as we have been promoted to Pilot Officers from Acting Pilot Officers. It was a terrific party. The Station Commander was not there. We played all sorts of games and beat 1 Squadron every time. We were all a bit tight and Caesar (Squadron-Leader C. B. Hull, DFC, killed during the Battle of Britain) was at the top of his form, rolling about the floor on Johnny's back biting his ears! They are a superb couple.

I could not do much cockfighting myself as I have only just had the plaster taken off my wrist. We all finished up in the Sergeants' Mess.

I have been made Squadron Adjutant. I shall enjoy it as it should not reduce my flying time and will be good training. I sent for Caesar to report to me just as he was about to fly today, just to annoy him. We are flying together this afternoon for the first time. No doubt he'll pay me back. He's a wizard pilot.

I've bought a baby dachshund – he's called Fritz.

March

As I write, I hear news on the wireless of snow and rain and wind in Essex. How is the house and the garden? It is much warmer here today and we have two daffodils out. I have just heard that Willy Graham Browne died today and that Marie Tempest is going on with the show tonight as usual. How astounding! What terrific vitality she has! And so brave. May I bring Fritz for Easter? He will not make maps on the carpet now.

They have formed two new squadrons here. Things seem to be buzzing in the Air Ministry.

March

I have just flown with Caesar. We were meant to do some instrument flying together, taking it in turns to be under the hood. But of course, the moment we had taken off, we had no intention of doing anything except try to frighten each other. It was a lovely cloudless day and we hovered over the Sussex Downs at about ten thousand feet.

Ever since I have been here, I have felt behind the others and have been slower in my training … particularly in landing and taking off in formation. I think really that I am a little frightened. I have never admitted it to you before. But there it is. Knowing Caesar is making a difference. I can't quite say why, but he seems to give me confidence.

You see, 43 has a reputation throughout the Service for their formation flying. We fly tucked in so close that there are only a few inches between us … six inches is the average. After flying with Caesar yesterday I think my fear has almost gone.

He started off by doing a falling leaf in our old Hart, which I had never done before. Then he tried to do a bunt but failed. I don't know whether you know what that is, but it usually tears the wings off an aeroplane. He was frightened that the Hart just wouldn't take it.

We did inverted spins and rocket loops, but I have such confidence in him that I wasn't frightened once. You know how he loves flying. I think it is his only passion. Frankly, I think that if he had to choose between a girl and a Fury he would take the Fury. You know that he is a boxer. But his hands aren't the least bit tough. Although they are usually bruised and grazed from the rough houses we have in the mess. He's such a polished pilot that he takes risks that I would never dare attempt.

I tried to frighten him when I took over. I did loops and rolls without any fear. I have always been over cautious about this when Caesar was about because he's so good at it. But yesterday, those loops and rolls and spins were something to write home about.

It is fun having him to talk shop to. When we landed we hit each other very hard on the back and he said, 'Wizard,' which he says to everything. Caesar and Prosser Hanks have threatened to change seats in the air, flying the same Hart. It sounds impossible and I only hope they won't try.

March

Caesar and Prosser have done it! They took off in an Audax yesterday and said that they were going to change seats in the air. We were not impressed and when they landed, in different seats, we said that they must have come down somewhere and changed. We baited them and Johnny Walker insisted that they must do it again over the aerodrome to prove it. They staggered off to about 5,000 feet over our heads, and from the manoeuvres the aircraft was doing it was plain to see that they were really changing. Johnny, Walker and I were rather frightened in case one of them fell out. After a time, the aircraft flew normally and they landed.

It was quite true. They had changed seats in the air. It was pretty hair raising when you consider that they had to take their parachutes off to do it.

11 June 1937

I think I can wangle out of church next Sunday and come down to Boytons on Friday. May I bring Caesar for a quiet weekend? He needs one before he performs at the Hendon Air Display the following Saturday. They have chosen him to do the individual aerobatics. We rag him about it and say, 'God, you're getting so conceited.' But nothing could be less true.

1 Squadron are going to do the flight aerobatics, so Tangmere is well represented as usual.

You will like Caesar. His voice is odd. It's more like a croak. As if he's got a very sore throat. We tell him to pull his voice out of his boots. He's one of the cleanest people I have ever known. Immaculately dressed. I've never heard him say a nasty word about anyone.

He's really a marvellous person. If there is a wet pilot in the squadron the others don't like, Caesar will concentrate on him and help him. He's got a talent for drawing the weak chap into the Air Force picture. He's a strange mixture. Tough, as a boxer, a wonderful pilot and yet he's full of superstitions. He hates flies and slugs and worms. If we throw a worm at him he just shouts, 'Help' and runs.

Maybe his dislike for insects is because, while he was being born, a swarm of bees settled on the end of his mother's bed.

We've got a little garden in front of our hangar and I am in charge of it. A few days ago I found a worm and I threw it at him. He said, 'Right, John, you wait until I see you in the air. I'll menace you.' He did the next day. I was flying by myself in the morning and he came and attacked me and did all sorts of aerobatics all round me, so close that I kept getting into his slipstream.

I am so glad you like Rhys-Jones. He is a very fine type. I shall fly up with Caesar and land at Debden. Can you send the car?

16

I remember Caesar walking into the house for the first time and conquering us with his personality and charm. He was the essence of a fighter pilot. The bomber pilot is a different man, with the reticence and silent loyalties of a sailor. But the fighter pilot is as independent as an eagle and he is noisy. He leaps where the bomber pilot walks.

Caesar was a South African, but his energies were controlled by a tenderness of heart which might have emerged from an old, rather than a young civilisation. His face was so lively with laughter and intelligence that one did not realise for a long time that it was a very average face as far as features go. He moved quickly as if, accustomed to flying, he was rather impatient with the slow tempo of his feet. Like most of the pilots who loved the Service in pre-war days he had little life beyond the Air Force. Girls were toys to be fondled in the back of a car, but forgotten. He was married to the RAF. Caesar was a boxer, but in the rough and tumble games which were played in the mess, his hands were never angry. In the quiet of his room, he read long serious books, mostly Winston Churchill. He was a strange mixture. At night he looked beneath his bed, imagining that somebody might be hiding there. He wore a scarf which had belonged to him since the day he first flew. He would not fly without it and one afternoon when his CO hid it, as a joke, Caesar refused to go near his aircraft.

He was impatient with doctors and illness. John wrote to me a little time after I first met Caesar:

He's always breaking a bone or something. He broke his leg, as I told you, and the doctors told him that he must keep the plaster on another week. About six days ago he came to my room in despair and we cut the plaster off with a fork and a nail file. He leapt about like a schoolboy, he was so pleased to be free of it. When he went to the doctor this morning, he told him that it was itching so badly that he had taken the plaster off an hour or two before. The doctor believed him. He examined the leg and passed Caesar fit.

When Caesar gave John a bottle of whisky for Christmas he sent it with a note that said, 'Try and drink it in one swig and kill yourself.'

There were other sides to him. He adored his sister and turned his back on the pubs, during his leave, to stay with an uncle and aunt who lived near Guildford. The ground Crews and sergeant pilots loved him.

I think one may say, quite simply, that Caesar did not know what meanness meant, nor weakness. But he was tolerant of both faults in anyone else. Injustice surprised him and left him slightly embarrassed.

I suppose that it was a godsend that he became John's friend because, watching them at a distance, I saw John improve and grow towards fresh goodness under his influence.

But all this seems to suggest nothing but seriousness. Those weekends, when I put aside my biographies and gave the house over to John and Caesar and any others who came, were gay from beginning to end. They knew how to make a party, because they didn't consciously try. There I was, in the last of my thirties, hanging on to the running board of a car while we flew down the lanes of Essex, trying to reach the pub at Thaxted 'before they closed'. And there is a small scar on my ankle, as a souvenir of the night when I climbed over the wall of Downing College, to end the

University Air Squadron dinner in the rooms of some of the pilots. It was a policeman's torch, flashed on my crumpled white shirt, that made me jump the 10-foot wall and run into a fog.

17

The shadows of the war were slowly coming over all this. Perhaps I did not see them then, but as I read the letters which John wrote to me from Tangmere, a phrase here and there builds up the story. During the winter of 1936 he wrote to me:

Did you realise that it was me waving to you before lunch on Tuesday? I kept my promise and did not come too low. But I could see a smile on your face as you leant from your bedroom window … There is nothing new or any different here, except that my room is in a mess … having gas-proof windows put in. Sir Edward Ellington came down to interview us all. With what object I do not know. You must come and see the Tangmere silver and gold one day. We have more trophies than any other squadron in the Service. Our next guest night, you must make an effort … I motored over to Brighton on Saturday night and dined alone at Sweetings and then returned here. No one can understand that side of me … They think I've got a little job I pop into bed with at Brighton.

Caesar broke an ankle playing rugger on Saturday and is now in hospital for two weeks, nearly dead with boredom … I am flying well and working hard. I sold my old dinner jacket for £1 to an Australian here.

It has been a fine weekend, but very cold. Mac came down to spend the weekend with me, as everyone else was away.

How is your health? I hope you are getting better and will be quite fit for Christmas. Caesar asked me to go with him on a fishing trawler for a week at Christmas, as crew, living on fish and costing nothing. Poor boy has no money and he wants to go away. But can you see me in a trawler, in mid-winter, sleeping on the floor wrapped in blankets! I wouldn't do it for anything, not even with a Greek Goddess!

In January of the new year, John wrote again:

I had dinner in the *Courageous* on Sunday. Very entertaining but too much gin. There is a plaque on the flight deck of the *Courageous* where Hank (Group Captain J. W. C. More, OBE, DFC) landed in a Fury to the amazement of the Navy. It has never been done before.

It is odd how one sometimes wishes to get away from people for a change. Last night, instead of going out with the boys, as is usual on Saturday night, I stole away in the car by myself to Brighton and had a very good dinner. Then I sat in the stalls and saw Shaw's 'Candida'. It was brilliant. Ann Harding, Edward Chapman and Stephen Haggard (exceptionally good). And Athene Seyler. I really loved it and I've lost my heart to Ann Harding. Today I have had my first exercise for three months. I hired a horse for two hours and with four others we rode over the downs. It rained. I enjoyed my hot bath when I returned.

29 March 1938

I flew with two others up to Grantham for morning tea and petrol, and then on to Catterick for luncheon. After lunch we flew back and arrived here by teatime. Six hundred very pleasant miles. About

Easter ... I shall try to fly down to see you but I think I will have little chance. We are so short of aircraft and it would mean that some of our pilots would have no flying for two days.

March or April 1938

We all loved having you down here for the sports. My ankle is still pretty sore, but the silver cups are in my room to help me forget it. Caesar won more than I did. But he took one good cup and pooled the rest of his prizes into a Rolls razor and gave it to me for a present.

Yes, it was Peter Townsend (now Wing Commander P. Townsend, DSO, DFC and bar. He was the second officer in 43 Squadron to bring down an enemy aircraft in this war) I meant. He used to be rather aloof, going to his room at night and avoiding our games and parties. But we are bringing him out of his shell. He is very shy and has no idea of his own courage. He thinks he will hate war if it comes. Caesar moans because there is no war. He reads Winston Churchill by the hour and knows all the answers. Peter is a different type. Very English on the surface. His brothers are in the Navy and Army and he was in torpedo bombers in the Far East. He's the greatest gentleman I have ever met in the Service. He surrounds himself with armour, but I am slowly breaking through. We are becoming friends. You will like him when you know him more. He's got the sort of face you notice immediately he comes into a room.

25 June 1938

Well Gatwick is over. It's a pity it was so windy and bumpy, but we seem to have done our stuff pretty well. Have you seen the photographs and write-ups in the *Express*? No. 1 Squadron are teasing us like hell. Most of them were there and I think they are a bit jealous! Poor Caesar in the flight aerobatics! I was so sorry for him, breaking formation in the first loop. It wasn't his fault. I was amazed how he got back into formation for his roll.

We had a pretty tough struggle in the line abreast flypast. It was so bumpy and a Fury gets thrown about like hell in that sort of weather. I was lucky to be next to Dickie Bain in the centre. Poor old Jack Sullivan was near the end and had hell. I wish the weather had been better. We usually fly closer than we were able to. Thank you for the telegram of congratulations. I *was* proud of the squadron and being a member of it. I was not very impressed by Al Williams, the American, in his Grumman Hell Diver. It was a big line. But he's a good chap.

The two Huns put up the best show of the display. The aerobatics and inverted flying were Wizard, and the chap in the glider put up a beautiful flying performance. I've never seen such polished glider flying before. Not that I've seen much anyway. We asked the Germans to come over to Tangmere with Al Williams for dinner, but they couldn't make it.

1 January 1939

I got a little drunk on New Year's eve at a dance. It was in fancy dress and I went as Hitler. Can you imagine it?

16 January 1939

I have had a depressing week. Charles Douglas, (Alexander Charles Douglas, killed while flying at Tangmere, 14 January 1939) who spent last weekend with me, was killed in an aircrash on Monday. It's horrible how these things happen every year. I have taken three days leave, to avoid the funeral. Some of the bulbs are showing through the earth, but no aconites. There are a number of good shaped Christmas roses, but they are a bad colour.

3 *August* 1939

What a flap! At ten o'clock on Tuesday night the order came through to mobilize. I was up all night working like a beaver, calling up all the reservists and people on leave. By tonight we should be complete. We just sit around, not allowed to fly or leave the camp until we get an order to move or go up and attack. It's quite exciting. As I write this I am wearing the most amazing anti-gas clothing. Our fighting with the French starts on Tuesday and finishes on Friday night.

23 *August* 1939

I can give you no news of when I can get away. At the moment we are busy preparing for another war scare. Thursday night is supposed to be zero hour. Tonight I go to bed early as I fly all night tomorrow.

27 *August* 1939

Your letter gives me great courage. It calmed me when I needed it. Everybody here is remarkably gay and everything is being taken calmly. Personally, I am not worried about it a bit. I believe in myself and I know what capabilities I have and how to use them without being overzealous. I wish I could see the garden.

1 *September* 1939

It is ten o'clock on September 1 and I have just heard the horrible news. I am quite calm and we are all ready. If you could get down here some time we could talk and laugh. I wish you would take Fritz. I can't very well ask Mummy to have him in London. He would be a nuisance here, with gas, etc. Don't worry about me. I'll fix them.

18

3 September 1939

You can't expect a letter. I am working terribly hard. We were all in the mess when the news came through. We were drinking beer. Caesar said something about old Umbrella Chamberlain and that we had to admire the organisation of the Germans in the way they have gone into Poland. He says we will lose for certain if we are governed by people like umbrella C who believe that the tanks and the guns that go down the Wilhelmstrasse are really made of cardboard and thin plywood. I couldn't agree with him more. Johnny Walker was with us too. Caesar jumped from one foot to the other and said, 'Wizard.' He thinks I'll be shot down. He said, 'Never mind, John, you'll be killed early on.' He punched me in the back and laughed. But then we were silent. You could have heard a pin drop. We had to go back to readiness immediately, in case anything happened. So far it hasn't. We had our midday meal beside our aeroplanes.

Well, it's the war we have been expecting so we can't grumble. I don't feel the least bit afraid or even fussed, but I feel tired. What are you going to do? Are you going to stay on in the house?

John's questions were answered before his letter arrived. It seemed the natural thing for me to offer myself to the Air Ministry straight away and I left for London within an hour. But this is not my story. All I wish to say is that, for all the frustration, dullness and piles of paper, I would not have had it otherwise. I was able to watch the growth of the battle, even if it was only on maps and in reports. But, during those early months of the war, when we slept in a cellar with the rivets of a sewer for our coat hooks, through terrible long hours of work, we lived near to the miracle which was being performed outside. There was a thread of dedication in our work and we felt that we were at least a small part of that miracle when we stood in the war room and read the first combat reports that came through ... scratchy stories of battles, written by the pilots on sheets of green paper, when they were so tired that they could barely write. In their combat reports they wrote the story of their own heroism in phrases as simple as the psalms. And, like the psalms, they seemed to come from another world.

19

On 30 January 1940, when the war in the air was still young – while the German pilots were still too careful to attack more than fishing smacks or lifeboats loaded with supplies, Caesar Hull brought down the first enemy aircraft for his squadron, off the East Coast. John told me the story in a letter:

31 January 1940

I am very tired. We have had three days of great activity, with some success. You know I told you yesterday that Caesar, with another pilot, intercepted and shot at a German bomber. During the attack a bullet hit his aircraft behind the cockpit and went through the aircraft, doing no damage. The German news claimed that Caesar had been shot down. Perhaps you heard it.

Yesterday, Caesar and the *same* pilot, in the *same* aircraft – intercepted and shot down a bomber ten miles out to sea. There were no survivors.

Don't you think that is good! The same pilots, in the same machines (one of which the Germans claim to have shot down) got their revenge for the one bullet (which did no damage) by shooting down a Heinkel 111 the next day. We are all as pleased as Punch.

At the moment I am writing on my knee in a caravan. Caesar sends his love and hopes you are not as cold as he is. He says, 'Tell Hector to use his influence on Hitler and ask him to come and bomb something.'

Thirteen days later, the three friends, Peter Townsend, John and Caesar, came into their own as fighter pilots. They were the leaders of three formations that brought down three German aircraft off the East Coast, within the space of five minutes. John wrote to me:

Birdie Saul (Air Vice-Marshal R. E. Saul, CB, DFC, who was then in command of No. 13 Group) has just telephoned the CO. He was away, because his wife is having a baby. So I had to take the call, being Adjutant. Birdie Saul congratulated me and said that the Hun I claimed earlier in the day had been confirmed.

The bodies of two of the crew were already on the way to us at Acklington for a military funeral. One German was picked up in the sea and one was washed ashore. The medical officer asked me if I would like to go and see the corpses when they arrived at the mortuary. But I said no.

I'll begin at the beginning.

Last night we slept at Dispersal Point for early morning readiness. We had cold kippers brought over for breakfast, cold and unpleasant because we are so far from the mess.

These kippers are unique. One morning George Lott had just swallowed half his kipper when we suddenly scrambled. He was told to go up above all cloud. He couldn't climb above 29,500 feet: that was as high as the bloody thing would go. He says that it is the highest a kipper has ever flown in its life and how surprised its mother would be if she ever knew.

This morning was misty and damp with occasional showers and low clouds down to five hundred feet. You know how depressing this part of the country can be, with the slag heaps and the wind coming in from the North Sea.

Peter and his section were ordered off and told to patrol South Shields. Shortly after, both Caesar's sections and mine were also ordered off, Caesar to the mouth of the Tyne and me to the Faroe Islands. We were warned that there were enemy aircraft about presumably looking for our convoys. We flew around the Faroe Islands ... they are quite small, with a lighthouse and millions of birds. There was enough rain to keep the windscreen misty and make flying unpleasant. We found a small convoy after about half an hour and we were circling it when I saw three white splashes in the water, to one side of the centre ship. It was a small ship, with a sail and one funnel ... a fishing boat I suppose. I realised the splashes were from bombs and I looked up and saw an immense aircraft just below the clouds.

It was the first Heinkel I had ever seen and I just hoped that it wasn't one of ours. The Heinkels look quite like Ansons from underneath. Several times we have taken Ansons for Heinkels and only just realised in time. Much to the alarm of the Coastal Command pilots. But I was certain this time. It looked dark and ugly and I pulled up the nose of my Hurricane and pressed the tit. I hit him fair and square in the wings and fuselage. One of his engines stopped and bits of metal flew off. He then disappeared into some wisps of cloud. We circled round for a few seconds and my Number 2 (Eddie Edmonds, Flying Officer J. D. Edmonds, presumed killed 7 June 1940) said, 'I see the bastard.' He could see the crippled Heinkel in a gap in the clouds and he fired.

The Hun was now flying towards the English coast. I caught up and finished all my ammunition on him. He was burning well when he disappeared into the mist above the sea. My ammunition tanks were empty so I called up Eddy and set course for base.

All the troops were on the tarmac when we arrived. I thought that they had come out because they could see that my guns had been fired (the gun ports on an aircraft are covered with fabric which is naturally blown away when the first shot is fired). For a moment I thought that I had drawn the first blood for the day. But Peter had gone in before me. He had already landed, having brought down his first over Whitby in Yorkshire. It was a Heinkel also and it had crashed near a farm. Peter was obviously very excited, but modest. He just said, 'Poor devils, I don't think they were all killed.' As we were talking, news came over the R/T that Caesar and Frank Carey (now Wing Commander F. R. Carey, DFM and DFC and two bars. He rose from the rank of Sergeant Pilot to Wing Commander in two years) had shot down another near the mouth of the Tyne. They landed a few minutes later and Caesar was frightfully excited, saying, 'God! It was wizard. Frank and I did beam attacks from opposite directions and nearly collided.'

The crew of Caesar's Heinkel stood on top of the fuselage when their aeroplane landed in the water. It was so like Caesar ... he dived on them, but without firing, just to beat them up. They all jumped into the water and he was delighted. He kept on saying, 'It was wizard.'

152 Squadron are here also and they brought down one. They have only just formed so it was a terrific show for them. They only have Gladiators.

I was not absolutely certain of mine although we claimed it, until Birdie Saul rang through. I had given the position of the Hun over the R/T and one ship in the convoy had been diverted to look for the crew. Also a local lifeboat had put out. It was awfully hard luck on George Lott. We sent him a wire, telling him to listen to the six o'clock news. He was bloody annoyed at missing the Huns and he is coming back on the night train. He's so terribly keen I'm sorry he missed the show.

152 are arranging a party for us tonight.

Later

The party was a great success. Peter and Caesar did their wonderful La Cachita dance to the gramophone record we brought from Tangmere. It is a cross between a rumba and an apache dance and they throw each other all over the room, crash, bang! They jump over the tables and chairs while they are dancing. We drank eight bottles of champagne.

We then sang our old Air Force songs ... 'My mother comes from Norfolk', 'My brother Silvest' and 'Take the Piston Rings out of My Stomach'. Poor old Caesar tried to join in. Have you ever heard him sing? It is a horrible business. He simply cannot keep tune. We just stopped and looked at him and he went scarlet. He was always the same in the old days in the little church at Tangmere. I remember one Sunday when he was in front and we all began to sing 'Abide with Me'. He couldn't resist it and he began to sing. He was so loud and out of tune that somebody leaned over and touched me on the shoulder and said, 'Tell Caesar to pipe down.' I poked him in the back and told him and he went red to the back of his ears.

Caesar is slightly religious. He always says his prayers and I think he would like to sing hymns. But he has no idea of being in tune, which is extraordinary because he has such rhythm in his flying.

I admire him so much about this side of him ... I mean his saying his prayers. When we were at camp at Watchet, we shared a room. After he had done all his little fusses, like looking under the bed and in the cupboard, he just laughed and told me to look under mine. 'You never know, there might be some feeneys about.' Then he knelt by the side of his bed and said his prayers.

You know that Caesar has invented a *La Cachita* attack in the air. He calls out *La Cachita* over the R/T to Peter and follows with a noise like a machine gun. Then Peter calls back, '*Himmel, Himmel! Achtung! Schpitjeuer*'. Then they make an astern attack in echelon with three aircraft. They each come down and take on their opposite number. It is wonderful listening to it over the R/T. Caesar makes it all sound very exciting with his *La Cachita* nonsense.

Next day, John told me, Peter went to inspect the wreckage of the Heinkel at Whitby. Afterwards, he went to see his German prisoner in hospital and took him cigarettes. John added, 'We are contributing to buy wreaths for the dead ones.'

20

Pilots may know how to fight, but they are equally whole-hearted in their pleasures. One of their talents is in being able to turn quickly from their battles in the skies to their pleasures on the earth. Again and again through John's letters, one finds him describing the long dreary job of the day, or a combat with an enemy … and then telling of some foolish party or some lively jaunt into the neighbouring town. In one letter he wrote:

We now have to protect the coastal convoys. It is dull and very tiring as we fly only a few feet off the water. But we are all enjoying ourselves here. I wish I could fly you over the mountains so that you could see the colours while the sun is on them: deep purple, brown and green, changing the whole time as the sun moves. At sunset it is astounding.

On Wednesday, George Lou, Peter and Caesar and I went into Newcastle to see 'The Importance of Being Earnest'. We went round afterwards and I took George and Peter and Caesar to John Gielgud's dressing room. John was a little shy and then Jack Hawkins came in and Caesar asked him how he swallowed all those crumpets. Caesar still kept up that shocking laugh. He croaked at Jack H and Jack H laughed, and it all went with a swing. Then we walked back to the hotel with John Gielgud and joined the whole company at supper. It was fun. The good days in Essex all came to life again (both John Gielgud and Gwen Ffrangcon-Davies have houses in Essex near to mine. John's reference is to Sundays when we met before the war). Gwen was there and so very kind to us. I felt rather homesick. George and Peter and Caesar had never been behind a stage in their lives before and I felt a bit grand being able to show them something new. They were thrilled. Gwen and John could not have been kinder, and Edith Evans. I sat next to Edith Evans at supper. Celia Johnson had made old Caesar hot beneath the collar during the play, but she wore glasses at supper and didn't take the slightest notice of him. I suppose she was shy or tired. Jack Hawkins was absolutely superb.

There is a plot on the board to chase. We have had a bad week. Two people killed and four broken aircraft. No one you know. It is really terribly cold here, 20 degrees below. I did six hours flying yesterday and I am tired out. Flying over the water at mast height, beside the ships, so we can look up instead of down is not much fun. The Hun comes over in bad weather and that is why we fly low, so that we can look up and see him if he pops out of the clouds.

Gwen Ffrangcon-Davies is an absolute pet … I wrote the first part of this letter and kept it, supposing there might be something to add. Well, there is. A parcel arrived this afternoon, addressed to me. It was a box and inside were four little parcels, in tissue paper. There were labels, one for Caesar, one for Peter, one for George and one for me. I opened mine and found a split muffin, tied together with tinsel string. Inside was a piece of red flannel cut into the shape of a heart, stitched into the lower half of the muffin. She had gone to all that trouble. God, she's a nice woman. I think she is really one's friend.

We all hung them in our bedrooms. Peter and Caesar want to go to Edinburgh, if the wicked enemy gives us a chance, to see Gwen again. Caesar says that she is wizard.

There is an awfully nice Mrs Widrington near here, five miles away, who allows us to shoot. George Lott and I go. They are absolutely nice people. Mrs W, her husband and a son. One realises how much they must hate all this – the noise of the aeroplanes. But they play up very well and take it in their stride.

In looking over the letters of three years ago, one suddenly realises what vast changes have come to administration within the Air Force since the war began. In the days of which I am writing, fighter pilots had also to do the work of adjutants. And there were not many intelligence officers to write down the result of the combats. John was still adjutant of his squadron and when he returned from his dreary vigils over the sea or from a battle, he had to sit down at a desk and cope with reports, files and letters.

One of John's letters reveals how far the Service has travelled in those three years. He wrote of 152 Squadron which had been fighting with biplanes since the squadron was formed.

152 are just being equipped with Spitfires. They think they are one up on us. But both Caesar and Peter have tried one today and there was a most amusing incident. They took off a few minutes after each other and circled the aerodrome and then joined formation. In full view of the whole aerodrome, they did a loop and a roll, in close formation. Their CO Freddy Shute (Squadron-Leader F. Shute, lost a month afterwards, flying out to sea in a Gladiator in bad weather), was angry but charming.

You can imagine what our ground crews were like. We have had our Hurrybugs since December 1938, and we still think they are the tops. Caesar and Peter still feel the same after their line shooting in the Spitfires. But the ground crews were even more excited than we were. It might have been a racehorse stable with rival trainers. They were jumping with joy when they saw the way Caesar and Peter put those Spitfires in their place. It may seem all nonsense, but I wouldn't change over if they asked me.

We went into Newcastle and did a pub crawl because, to be quite frank, Caesar and Peter rather felt that they had shot a line.

21 February 1940

Last night I had the first crash I've had since I've been in the Service. I am very lucky to be alive.

We were night flying and it was a pitch black night. Something went wrong with my motor soon after I took off. I was terrified, as I was too low to bale out and I knew that I must crash. I have told you, I think, how strong our Hurricanes are. My being alive now is proof of that all right.

It happened very quickly. I kept the aircraft straight and my speed as far as I could see at 100 mph. I couldn't put down the flaps. I just hit the top of a haystack which broke off half my propeller and sent me bouncing up into the air again, then a telegraph pole was cut in half, clean as a whistle, with the top still hanging on the wires. Then into the side of a wood of larch trees. My head felt as if it had come off, and there was blood coming out of me everywhere. The noise was colossal. I was terrified I would burn and somehow got out and ran away from the wreckage. I then passed out on the side of a road. I came to just before they found me – Caesar and Eddie – it took a long time. Caesar's first remark was, 'God, he's alive. John, you twirp. I thought you were dead. I've just been to your room and pinched your electric razor!'

They were sweet to me then and helped me to the car and sick quarters.

I look pretty bloody as I've broken my nose and my cheekbone and I'm bruised to hell. But I don't have to go to bed, and I'm getting a week's leave after the Doc has seen me tonight. I have had to wait in case I am concussed.

We looked at the wreckage today. It's amazing. There is practically nothing left except the cockpit. I cut down a nice piece of the wood – 36 trees.

I'll wire you when I'm coming South.

Two years or so afterwards, John said to me, 'I have not been an expensive pilot to the country. That Hurricane is the only loss to my debit. I have never, in all my years in the Air Force, burst a tyre or damaged a wing tip. I think perhaps people thought that I was too careful ever to become a good fighter pilot.'

21

Early in March of 1940, John's squadron was moved north to patrol over the Orkneys and to help to protect the Fleet at Scapa Flow. But it was a dull business because the Germans held back and did not take advantage of the target for some time. He wrote to me:

We are billeted in the Station Hotel, run by Dan Sutherland and his wife Elsie. Like most Scots, once they like you, they make you feel at home. But there is little else. The war is asleep on this piece of earth. I have a day off and I have come away by myself to sit and watch the birds. Eggs everywhere. It is my birthday, a fact that nobody seems to have remembered. Twenty-seven years old. Well, there it is. There are kingcups growing in the river, near the sea. I did not think they could. I have picked a few for my room. I feel thoroughly depressed. I would like to go away to a new and decent part of the world and use my brain. I have bought a bottle of champagne and I am going to drink it with Dan. I am well and calm, but depressed because I believe Caesar is going.

Last week I drove down the coast, past Hemsdale, to Dunrobin. I took George Lott and the Duchess of Sutherland gave us a very good lunch. She is handing over most of the house as a hospital. We came back through lovely country. I would love to stay in one of those fishing lodges, on the side of the mountain, looking down to the clear river below. Now, of course, they are all empty and cold looking as this is a prohibited area. I long to have more meals in houses with people out of uniform. Each evening I walk along the beach and climb on the rocks, jumping from one to the other. I can find nobody to share the pleasure of it with me.

Caesar and Peter refuse to take a day off in case anybody else gets the Huns before them. George ordered them off for a week's leave, but they came back after three days in case they were missing anything.

Life was quiet and cold on the northern tip of Scotland. It was spring, with little darkness and long hours of flying. When John came south in April 1940 he confessed that he was bored. For three days he walked about the garden. Even for me, with nothing more exciting than a desk job in Whitehall, leave was a disturbing and strange interruption. John had more reason for feeling restless. It was already impossible to believe in the illusion of relaxation. I suppose that we were all on the war machine by then and it was not easy to get off. On the evening of the third day we were sitting before the fire, just before going to bed, when the telephone bell rang. It was a call for John from the north of Scotland. The war had truly begun for 43. Caesar broke the news. The Huns had sent ten aircraft to bomb the fleet at Scapa Flow a few hours before. It was their first attempt at a big raid and it failed. 43 intercepted the Heinkels some ten miles off the Orkneys and gave them hell. At least five were shot down. Both Peter Townsend and Caesar had got one each and, judging by the shouting and abuse over the telephone, Caesar had found everything as wizard as ever. George Lott told me the story some time after. One Heinkel had actually landed on the flare path. George had listened in to the astonishing conversation over the R/T, one voice saying, 'Heinkel passing over aerodrome at 200 feet.' And the other protesting, 'Are you sure. Are you sure it is not a Hudson?' Then the bewilderment of the German crew who thought they were landing on the water at Scapa Flow and were so certain of this that they took off their boots and threw their rubber dinghy on to the ground.

All this came later. John did not wait for details after the telephone call. The fiasco of leave was over: he was off next morning, arranging to fly north again.

22

Even in the brief hours of his flight back to Scotland, John missed 'another party'. The story must be told for it reveals the spirit with which 43 was taking its place in the front line. Peter Townsend has written it down for me:

It was the afternoon of a lovely day, 10 April. The sky and sea were very blue. There were scattered clouds and isolated rain storms which would give very little cover to a snooper. Caesar's flight were released from duty and he and some others were playing tennis. My flight was at thirty minutes notice and was the last of five flights available for action. So I went into the town with Eddie, to do some shopping.

The siren sounded, just as we were buying some things. We ran to the aerodrome which was a mile away, and arrived at our Dispersal Hut, hot and flustered. George Lott was already there. He had been sitting in his office when he saw a lot of chaps rushing past the window. He had telephoned Ops, to see if there was anything doing. When they told him that there were some Huns about he said, 'Can we go?' Much to my annoyance. we found that our flight (B Flight) had only three aircraft which were serviceable. Several had been damaged when we brought down the five Germans in the blitz off Scapa Flow. Then Caesar arrived, with some others in his flight (A Flight). They were still wearing their tennis kit, shirts, flannels and rubber shoes. There were only a few of their pilots as the others had gone off for the day. It was a case of my flight having the pilots and A Flight having the machines. There was a rather heated discussion and then we arranged a compromise.

As we flew out towards the islands, we saw one Hun. We gave the Tallyho in one bellow, over the R/T.

The Hun might have heard us, he turned so steeply away and made for a small bank of cloud. George Lott got there first and gave him a burst just before he got into the cloud. Then Caesar showed his independence. He opened the throttle full out and drew away from me. Then he tore into the Hun who was then dodging in and out of cloud. Now it was a matter of each man for himself. We jostled and dodged each other as we tore in behind the Heinkel and every now and then there would be a yell of, 'Look out! For Christ's sake, you nearly hit me.' I can remember coming in with another Hurricane dangerously close above me. The rudder and fin of the Heinkel were wobbling and his whole fuselage was riddled. We told the boys not to fire any more because we saw that he was finished and we wanted, if possible, to bring them back alive.

Chapter Twenty-Two

Caesar and I flew in close to him, one on each side and I could see the horrible mess in the rear cockpit: It was a sad and beastly sight. But we were elated then and did not see it that way. The riddled aircraft with its flapping empennage, three terrified figures in the front of the aircraft. The pilot, his fair hair blown by the slipstream which was coming through his shattered windscreen, leaning forward and trying to urge his powerless machine to fly. His two companions making hopeless signs of surrender and despair. We just answered them with two fingers and an upturned thumb as we pointed towards the coast which was thirty miles away, in the hope that they would make it.

They didn't. The pilot brought his aircraft down to sea level and, pump-handling the control column he brought the great Heinkel to rest.

The fuselage broke in half immediately and the after end sank. One wing broke off and, tipping crazily in the air for a second, it slithered below the surface.

Three figures struggled clear of the sinking wreckage. They began to swim *backstroke,* in that icy water, towards the coast. The seven of us circled round and some of us transmitted to get a wireless fix of our position, so that they might send out a launch to rescue the Huns. But none came.

We resumed our formation and flew back. I can still see the agony and despair of the last minutes of those Huns. We were indifferent to it then, when we saw them. We knew quite well that many of us would have to endure just as much before the war finished.

23

On 9 May, John brought down his second aircraft, over the sea, 40 miles out. It was a Dornier Flying Pencil, the first of its type to be shot down off the British coast. He wrote to me two days afterwards:

I did not have a minute to telephone you on Thursday after my success. It was most exciting, and a new type, which was pleasing.

Well, let me begin at the beginning. Caesar left us on Thursday morning to go with his squadron (Caesar Hull went with the first Gladiator squadron to Norway. The story of his brilliant service was told in a series of articles by Victor McClure in *Blackwoods*, and in his book *Gladiators over Norway*). I can't tell you where but he won't have to go to the frigidaire for his ice. I felt bloody browned off about his going. We have done everything together since I joined the squadron. He was excited, of course, and quite fearless and full of all his theories on how to turn out the Hun.

Two hours after he left us, we had to take off. It was my first job as commander of the flight because I have taken Caesar's place. Also, you must remember that I had never flown with any of the chaps before, as it is A Flight and I was with Peter in B Flight. We were to patrol the aerodrome below cloud while another flight had to patrol above. The cloud was grey and thick. We were told that enemy aircraft were coming from the west and that they were nearing the aerodrome. We had just got up to 3,000 feet when I heard the other flight give a Tallyho! I rather thought we were out of it. One Hun was already being fired on by the six aircraft above us and it was no use my joining in. We flew on under the clouds out to sea and I felt a bit peeved at not being able to fire my guns. I was about to turn back to base when I saw another Hun, a long, slim, green aircraft, flying beneath a cloud, hugging it and just staying enough in the open to be able to see the water. We must have been about forty miles out to sea. It was beautifully calm. I was terribly lucky because I was in a perfect position to open fire with a full deflection shot, almost the moment I saw him. Unfortunately, I was out of range with my first burst and I think that I missed. He tried to climb back into cover of the cloud, but I got him with my next burst before he disappeared. It was terrific. I blew his nose right off. I must have killed the pilot. It burned furiously and dived into the sea and exploded. A terrible but a wonderful sight. Three people had jumped out of the rear gun position and I saw them fall from about 800 feet into the sea. I could not see the aircraft after it crashed into the water. Only a column of fire and black smoke. I saw one of the Germans in the water. I noted my position and flew back to base.

I honestly did not care a bit. I hate their guts now, after so many of my friends have been killed. I found that I took this one in my stride without a tremor. But I still feel quite sick when I am on the ground, before I take off. I suppose, this is some kind of fear. Once I am in the air this vanishes and I become excited instead. But I am always pleased when I land. If you go down to the house on Sunday, please see if Norman has remembered to plant out those sweet williams which were growing in the greenhouse. I expect the garden and the South of England are heavenly now. Tulips and bluebells. I expect everything is beautifully green, even the hedges and trees. I cannot describe the bleakness of everything here. The only flowers I have seen were those kingcups in the river and a sign of wild irises, struggling for existence.

24

The English habit of being silent over grief or, indeed, any intense emotion, may be in the best tradition. But it leaves biographers in a quandary when they search through letters and find only bald phrases used to record grand or solemn experiences. John wrote to me, early in May, 'I am slowly losing all my friends in 43 and now I am the oldest member. Peter has been posted today to command a squadron in the south.'

Already, the war had been going on long enough to deplete the ranks of the squadrons which fought in the first battles. Pilots with experience were needed to form new squadrons. Others had been killed. And the new young tide of pilots was already flowing in. The strength of the Service was mounting towards a million, and even young officers like John were finding themselves alone and bereft of the friendships and collaboration which had made the peace days so gay, and flying so exciting.

John wrote:

Caesar is still in Norway, I suppose, with Batchy Atcherley. And now Peter has gone. I am pleased, for him as he has done so well with us. I know he will be magnificent with a squadron of his own. I think he is getting a DFC (Peter Townsend was awarded the DFC in May 1940). It will be the first DFC for our squadron. He is an extraordinary person. Do you remember how shy and self contained he was? It has all gone now. He loves his gay parties and the squadron worship him. He is the hero of the squadron to the ground staff. What a lesson one can learn from a person like that, in watching the way he works with the men. He never needs to be angry or tiresome, or even particularly firm with them. It just comes from inside him and I suppose they know a gentleman when they meet one. I have noticed it a lot when I have been censoring the men's letters, how they all think the world of him. I shall miss him. I bet he'll do the best of all of us in this bloody war. George Lott, Eddie Edmonds and I are becoming very good friends. Eddie used to be in the Fleet Air Arm. He has a brother in the Service also. Eddie has many of Caesar's characteristics. He is always laughing. The chaps love him. He's a good pilot and the greatest fun in the world on a party. We share a room in the hotel and I think that we are Elsie's pets. After we have been flying late into the night and come back dog tired we get the next morning off until one o'clock. Elsie and Dan Sutherland always wait up for us and give us a drink before we go to bed. And they have a great deal of work to do in the hotel. She usually wakes us up herself, fairly late next day, and *brings us our breakfast in bed.*

The war has taught me that these are really the great British people, who work hard and seem to have more to give people because of it. They are very fond of each other and completely unselfish. They are really marvellous to the whole squadron.

Did I tell you that they give us a bottle of champagne every time we shoot down a Hun?

We have at last got an adjutant, Stuart Cary. He has fitted into the squadron straight away. He is a charmer and already has the 43 spirit. We have had some pretty terrific parties with him. I think he will help George a great deal, which will allow him to fly more.

I am a lucky person, Hector. The squadron is really grand in spite of losing Caesar and Peter ... and now Frank Carey. He is getting a commission so he has to leave us. We are such a happy family and have such a wonderful team spirit. I sometimes think that other squadrons are a bit jealous when they see us all having fun together. When we all go on a party we usually take the sergeant pilots with us. They are grand chaps who have all been in the squadron for a long time and they have a tremendous respect for it and the officers. I think they will get commissions in time. In many ways I think they have an advantage over us because, being sergeant pilots first, they see every side of the picture and this should make them good officers.

I fly with a wizard little chap as my number 2. He used to fly with Caesar in the old days, so I have something to live up to. His name is Tony Woods-Scawen (Flying Officer C. A. Woods-Scawen, DFC, killed 2 September 1940). He's the biggest and smoothest flirt that I have yet come across. His room is surrounded with pictures of naked jobs much to the delight of Knockers North (Flight Lieutenant H. L. North, DFC, reported missing early in 1942), who is also in my flight and a bloody good type. He hails from New Zealand so you must meet him sometime. He has a tough time because he nearly goes mad if he is tickled. Naturally, when we are at dispersal and have nothing to do, we menace him the whole time and he gurgles and doubles up when we tickle him.

George and I are going into Thurso tonight to have a few drinks and some dinner. I think that the war in France is depressing him. It looks pretty bloody. I wonder whether it's the army's fault. I wish we had more squadrons there. Poor No. 1 Squadron must be having a pretty bloody time. I hear that dear old Laurie is missing. I must say that it will leave a gap in my life if I never hear his Irish laugh again. Do you remember how he used to cook sausages in the kitchen and yell to you, 'Heigh! The bangers are coming up like nobes! Laurie – Flight Lieutenant R. L. Lorimer – loved cooking great frying pans of sausages in my kitchen. His slang was unique. The phrase, 'The bangers are coming up like nobes' meant that the sausages were cooking like nobody's business.

The other Squadron, 605, is moving south tomorrow and we are told that we are getting a squadron from France. I cannot believe it. The squadrons can't be coming back yet unless, of course, they have had terrible casualties. I wish they would send us out there. I know that we'd do well. I hear that Dickie Lee has done wonders. You see how those boys, who were always looked upon as being the naughty ones, are doing so well. They needed a war to convince the old gentlemen in Whitehall. Do you remember that Dickie was almost given his bowler hat for low flying? That same low flying has apparently stood him in good stead.

I met some of the chaps from Walter Churchill's squadron (No. 3 Squadron was commanded by Flight Lieutenant, afterwards Group Captain Walter Churchill, DSO, DFC, killed at Malta, August 1942), and they were full of stories of Belgium. They all say Dickie did marvellously. In the first ten days of the German invasion of Belgium and Holland his squadron brought down between sixty and seventy Huns. Dickie was actually taken prisoner on the second day. On the first day he was wounded but he carried on. So like him. Next day he shot down two enemy aircraft and then he was caught by the German flak. He came down in a field and asked the way. The man told him to go to some tanks which were nearby and said that they were Belgians. Dickie was a bit of a sucker about this and, with a Belgian officer, he went towards the tanks, armed with a machine gun. The tanks turned out to be German so the machine gun was not much use. Dickie had an overcoat and the Huns did not realise that he was one of us. They popped him into a barn with some refugees.

Now comes the piece that is so like him. There was a high window in the barn. Dickie climbed up the wall to look out. Of course, he's a lucky blighter. There was a ladder beneath the window so he just climbed out and walked four miles, got a lift from some Belgians and he was back with the squadron to fight next day.

31 May 1940

A hurried note. We are to move back to dear old Tangmere today. To help in the evacuation from Dunkirk. I am taking off in about an hour. We have had little time to pack and we are all flapping a bit. The ground crews are delighted. They all love Tangmere and feel a bit resentful if anybody else is there. Crackers Carswell, our other New Zealander who crashed into the sea a month or so ago, has turned up today from hospital. When he crashed he went to the bottom of the sea and got out of his aeroplane. It must have been a bit much. He escaped, however, and one of the ships in the convoy he was protecting picked him up. He always sings those Maori war songs when he is a bit tiddly. They mean nothing to us so we call him Crackers. He is always washing his hands. He has a thing about cleanliness of his hands. He is delighted that we are moving as he hasn't had a crack at the Hun yet.

I have just heard from the Station Intelligence Officer that 605 Squadron were sent from here to cover the evacuation from Dunkirk. News has come through that they have lost nearly all their chaps on the first day, including their CO, George Perry (Squadron Leader G. Perry, commanding officer of 605. Missing since 31 May 1940). Such a charming person with a delightful wife.

I am ashamed to think I was the least bit sorry when I shot down my first Hun. There were so many good types in 605, and so many of them were my friends. Most of them are missing. It must be hell for the army in France.

25

On 5 June, we both had a respite of twenty-four hours ... myself from my files in Whitehall and John after playing his part in the astonishing moral victory of Dunkirk. It was a lovely day and we spent it in the garden in Essex. I have never known anybody as capable as John of losing himself in the experience in hand. I was silent and confused as I saw him walk into the house, change into some old clothes and then walk about the garden which he had helped to make and which he loved. He flew up to Debden in his Hurricane. Norman, our gardener, was so excited when I told him that John was arriving that he whistled – for the first time in my memory. 'It's a proud time for us,' he said, 'to have a hero coming home.'

At seven o'clock the evening before, John had returned from Dunkirk. The evacuation was over. Within twenty minutes of his arrival in the house he was walking about the garden, being a little overcritical and assuring me that I could quite easily pop down from London now and then to see that every possible inch of the ground was being used. The way he slipped from the role of fighter pilot back to the initial role of farmer's son was something which baffled me.

We dined and opened a bottle of claret to celebrate. Nowadays, when there is a tenant in the house, and the little objects one loved are cleaned and polished by alien, if sympathetic hands, that dinner we ate has a sentimental value. I am punctilious about a table and I like glass to be crystal clear and linen to be white. The ritual of a dinner is a pleasant form of behaviour to me. But all this belongs to the peace we have lost and may never have again. We made an effort over that dinner. The Greek silver ash trays were on the table. There were both port and madeira in the shadows behind us, beside fat red fruit. John had done well and his homecoming was to be celebrated.

So much had happened to him within himself, and there was so much quiet authority in his voice as he spoke, that I felt rather like a schoolboy listening to an old soldier. He had brought down two enemy aircraft at Dunkirk without even mentioning it when he spoke to me on the telephone the evening before.

43 Squadron had been ordered to help in the last days of the evacuation.

John told me the story afterwards and I wrote it down:

On the first day of our Dunkirk patrol, we took off from Tangmere while it was still almost dark. I shall never forget the mass of balloons all down the Thames, from London. We saw them in the distance, glittering in the morning light. They were so thick that they seemed to form a line, like silver battleships in the clouds, following the curves of the river.

We breakfasted at Manston and waited by our aircraft for the hour of our patrol. We were lying on the grass, reading the morning papers and I came upon the announcement that dear old George had got his DFC. There he was, lying next to me. And I realised, I don't know how – a sort of instinct – that, he had read it himself and had not said a word.

I congratulated him and he said, 'Christ knows what I got it for.'

I could not have been more pleased about any decoration. George is an extraordinary person and he deserves it. Behind that slow, quiet manner, there is a lot of courage and a good brain.

What was so nice was that when we returned from our patrol and he asked his batman to buy a DFC ribbon for his tunic, the twizzet bought a DFM ribbon by mistake. George wore it without even noticing until we told him.

On that first morning we made our way across the channel to Dunkirk. 43 flew 'above and behind.' We crossed the water above clouds and saw nothing of the evacuation which was going on below. But the smoke from the oil tanks at Dunkirk had reached us at Tangmere and we knew what to expect. We had smelled it in Sussex as we flew through it. You can fly from Brighton to Dunkirk on the smoke trail … just follow it and find Dunkirk at the other end.

All the harbour at Dunkirk seemed to be on fire with the black smoke from the oil dumps. The destroyers moved out of the pall of smoke in a most uncanny way, deep in the water and heavily laden with troops. I was flying at about 1,000 feet above the beach and the sea. And there I could see the *Brighton Belle,* and the paddle steamers, and the sort of cheerful little boats you see calling at coastal towns on Sunday. Hundreds of boats! Fishing boats and motorboats, and Thames river craft and strings of dinghies, being towed by bigger boats. All packed with troops, and people standing in the water and awful bomb craters in the beach, and lines of men and groups of people sitting down. Waiting, I suppose. And I could see rifles – stacked in threes. And destroyers going back into the black smoke. And wrecked ships on the beach: wrecked ships of all sizes, sticking out of the water. And a destroyer cut in halves by a bomb. I saw it! A Junkers 87 came low over the water and seemed to fly into the destroyer and drop its bomb. That was pretty terrible. It was shot down after, thank God. I saw the destroyer crack in two. And I saw parachutes coming down from wrecked aircraft, landing in the water and on the beach and on the land.

The first day we were patrolling, there were nine of my squadron, flying in a sort of oval-shaped route over the coast at between 10,000 and 20,000 feet. We flew two miles out to sea and then two miles inland. And suddenly, I realised that there were more aircraft flying than had come with us across the Channel. That was a bit disturbing! A squadron of Messerschmitt 109s had joined us and they were sharing our patrol peacefully, waiting to take their chance in getting a straggler. It was a bit shaking. I signalled to my CO when I recognised them. We had only come on bombers when we were in the North. Before the CO had time to give the order to attack a lone Messerschmitt dived down on him. The battle was on then. We picked our opponents, while two squadrons of our fighters flew low to protect the shipping. After avoiding several on my tail, for what seemed to be ages, I got on to one and opened fire. We chased about and lost height rapidly, coming down to 5,000 feet above the land. When he was diving I got in a steady burst and he crumbled up as if he were made of cardboard. He crashed in flames on a golf course.

I climbed up again and found that more German fighters, Messerschmitt 110s, also strangers to us, had joined in. I got on to the tail of one of them, which was firing at a Hurricane piloted by Crackers. I got so close that when I fired, his tail just blew off in mid-air. Crackers was on fire too. But he baled out and he was brought home by a destroyer two days afterwards.

Then I dived to the sea and made for home. I thought it was all right, but I made a silly mistake. In the heat of it all, I flew towards Calais instead of Dover. When I realised this, I turned and thought

I was alone for the journey across the Channel. But I looked back and saw that I was being followed by an enemy aircraft. We weren't more than three or four feet above the water. I zig-zagged to avoid his bullets. God was kind to me. We continued that mad, zig-zagging journey, so low over the smooth water, and he kept at me until I was eight miles or so from Dover. Then he turned and went home. It was our first combat with anything more than five aircraft … our first combat with any fighters. We got nine destroyed and six probable and we lost two.

The second night, John and I talked a little as we walked about the garden after dinner. It was a quiet evening, with only the noise of the hose on the cabbages and the barking of dogs and the sky brilliant with the ever-changing trellis of searchlights. John talked of the other pilots in his squadron. He had been trained with them and they had been his friends through all the danger and excitement. He was so proud of 43 and of his friends that he seemed to lose sight of the part he had played. He was uncertain from all that had happened which was strongest in his mind: his belief that he would live or his fear that he would die. I watched him, with the awe that an older man feels when a younger one talks of death. He swayed from one mood to the other. My own life seemed so petty, my complaints so trivial and my anxieties so selfish that I was silent. The fighter pilots were embarrassed by their own achievements. When the woman in our 'local' said to John, 'Please come down once, sir, in your uniform and let us see you' he obeyed, in a rather casual way. He was soon bored when we stood in the bar and he whispered to me, 'Let us go home.'

26

Next time John came on leave, his bag had reached seven. This was early in June of 1940, exactly six years after the day when he leaned over the railing of the ship and told me about his inferiority complex. He brought down his fifth, sixth and seventh enemy aircraft about the time when the German thrust was proceeding southwards. He wrote and told me the story:

It was a fine, clear summer day. Our squadron was ordered to patrol with nine aircraft on a line between Le Tréport, Abbeville and Amiens. We flew straight from our base on the English coast and made our landfall south of Le Tréport. Along the whole of our patrol line were smouldering villages, columns of black smoke and burning forests. Others had been there before us. As we turned to make for Rouen, where we were to land for lunch, a squadron of Messerschmitt 109 fighters attacked us from out of the sun. In a second we had broken our formation and each one of us engaged an enemy in a dogfight. There were more of them than of us and it was difficult to fire at one without being attacked by two others at the same time. I finished my ammunition, having fired at three of them. But the battle was too hot for me to follow and see if they crashed. I dived to the ground and made my way over the tree tops to Rouen which I found by following the Seine. When I landed I found that six pilots of my squadron had arrived before me. We were two short. Dickie Bain (now Wing Commander R. E. Bain. He commanded 43 Squadron before George Lott), the Station Commander, would not allow us to stay. The aerodrome had been bombed that morning and they were all preparing to move south.

So we had to take off again for an aerodrome thirty miles away. I had only ten minutes petrol left when we landed in a cut wheat field. While the ten men in the field refuelled our aircraft with only one petrol tanker between them, we climbed on to an American car and were driven at a hellish speed to a village. It seemed to be very peaceful, except for the motor cycles which flashed through on their way to Headquarters. There was a cart, with flowers and fruit and vegetables for sale. We were hot and thirsty. We talked of the combat, but not much of those who were missing. We just felt that they would turn up. We had a miserable lunch of cold sausage meat, brown bread, and quantities of watered down cider. We had no French money and we had to pay the angry madame with an English pound note.

We went back to the farm but the telephone wires had been cut. While the CO went back to the village to telegraph for orders, we stripped to the waist and lay in the sun, in the middle of the wheat field. We were seven, very white and clean, lying in the wheat. In one corner the Frenchmen were making a haystack and in the other corner some Cockney airmen were belting ammunition. We became thirsty again as we lay in the sun, but nothing could be done about it.

The Germans had advanced many miles while we were lying there. Our orders came. We were to patrol the same line, but two miles into enemy territory. We seemed to be very small ... only seven ... taking off. We flew in peace for ten minutes after arriving on our line and then the sky was filled with black puffs of smoke, like hundreds of liver spots. We dived and climbed and none of us was hit. When we turned at the eastern end of our patrol line the sky was fantastic. The black puffs of smoke from the anti-aircraft guns had woven weird patterns in the sky.

The guns stopped firing. We knew then that the German fighters were on their way. Coming towards us, in layers of twenty, were what seemed like a hundred of the enemy, looking like bees in the sky. Some were level with us. Some above. Some below. My CO climbed up with us to sixteen thousand feet and there, while we were being circled by all of those hungry fighters, he gave the order to break up and engage. Forty were bombers. They flew south: perhaps to bomb Rouen. I singled out a Messerschmitt 109 and had a very exciting combat with him. He was a good pilot and he hit me several times. We began to do aerobatics and while he was on his back, I got in a burst which set him on fire. He jumped out, but I did not see his parachute open. His machine was almost burned out before it hit the ground. There were scores of fighters about me, but I still had plenty of ammunition. I got on to the tail of another 109 and while I was firing at him two Messerschmitt 110s fired at me from either side. I continued to fire at the 109 which was badly winged. He suddenly stall turned sharply to the right, went into a spin and crashed straight into one of the other Messerschmitts which was firing at me.

I couldn't resist following them down. It was a wonderful sight. They stuck together in a sort of embrace of flames, until they were a few hundred feet above the ground. Then they parted and crashed, less than twenty yards apart.

I turned for home, flying as low as I could. Crossing the Channel seemed to take hours. I was wet through with sweat. I had been fighting at full throttle. The sea looked cool and it made me feel cooler. But I was afraid that I might be caught without ammunition and go into the sea. There were no beats to rescue me. Luck was with me for there was a mist above the sea. I flew in it for twenty minutes before I emerged into the sunlight again. I was lucky. The

Chapter Twenty-Six

Germans had lost me. I could see nothing but the sea and the English coast.

My wireless had been disabled so I could not inquire of my friends. At last I flew over land and very soon I was circling the aerodrome. I landed to find that I was the first home. My CO followed, having bagged two himself. We sat in the sun on the aerodrome for a long time, waiting for our other pilots. We searched the sky for them for what seemed an hour. But no more arrived. So we went to the Mess and we drank to ourselves and to them.

A few days later the newspapers announced that John had been awarded the Distinguished Flying Cross. His own account of the day in France suffered from under-statement. I learned afterwards that he had done very well. In the words of the official announcement he had shown 'a confident and offensive spirit' in the face of the enemy, and it was for this that he was to be decorated by the King. When he came on leave again he was much too interested in the crops and the garden to satisfy my questions. John was already a hero in my village, and Norman brought in the best of the vegetables and the first tomatoes as his own way of showing what he felt. He went so far as to break his silence once more and say, 'It's a proud time for us, sir, to have a DFC coming home.'

27

When John was awarded his DFC, the war was less than a year old and its full rigours and grief had not yet been felt throughout the country. But for the Royal Air Force these months already had the spaciousness of history. I remember how some of us talked of this in the garden when I was on leave in the summer of 1940. We went over to the aerodrome at Debden and walked into the officers' mess which we had all known so well in peacetime. But there was nobody whom we knew in the anteroom, so we walked away. A new generation of fighter pilots sprawled in the deep leather armchairs or turned the knob of the radiogram. They were the fresh force which had come in to take on the responsibilities of battle, for the ranks of the older pilots were already rather thin.

I wonder if it is possible to explain why, before the war, the Royal Air Force was so different in its social texture from any other service! A regiment knows itself within itself. People within a pocket of society, or embracing the code of any one profession are known in their own limited world. But the pilots of peacetime knew each other well, no matter whether they were serving in the cold north of Scotland or on the last edge of Cornwall ... in Ismailia or in Singapore, for that matter. They landed on each other's stations, as casually as people living in the same street might drop in on each other for a cup of tea. A pilot stationed at York might fly out to the Orkneys for lunch and back again the same day, bringing his catch of gossip with him. Next day he might fly to Aldergrove in Northern Ireland and return with news of the pilots he had seen there. Thus a great network of friendships was made, embracing all the length and breadth of the land.

When the war began, pilots did not view the battles within the confines of their own squadrons. They knew each other well, no matter how widely they were scattered. There was an organisation of telephones over the country and it was possible to gather the fragments of the great story into one. Bill had just telephoned from Hawkinge to say that George had escaped from France and that he had just walked into the mess, looking a little pale but full of beans. The adjutant at another station had just sent a signal to say that Peter had landed, a minute or two before, with two confirmed over the Cherbourg Peninsula. The older pilots were held together by these figments of news. The picture remained complete for them. But the news was often of death, so loneliness crept in. As the first year of the war ended these warriors felt a little estranged from the young. They handed on their tradition, but something was slowly being lost. It was the neighbourliness and intimacy which the Service had enjoyed when it was small.

At the beginning of the war the Air Officers Commanding Groups knew most of the squadron commanders by their Christian names. They were a comparatively small company, these pilots who led the first squadrons into combat, and although they may never have put the thought into words, there was between them something of the mystery and fealty that bound knights of old together. Even now, when the remnants of this company meet, they will forget the gold leaves of authority they now wear and something of the pre-war companionship will stir to life again. Old songs will be sung, old jokes will be recalled, and the conversation will be so full of nicknames and slang that strangers will not understand a word of it.

The young who come into the Air Force nowadays may live on the edge of this mystery and they may refresh their valour upon the example of these older men. But they can never know the full passion of belief that holds these survivors of the first battles so close together … these who are the few living, in the field of the numerous dead.

I have never found a sign of morbidity over death among pilots. When war was declared, few of them expected to live very long. John has since told me that he went to his room at Tangmere soon after the declaration and made his will. I have gone through the possessions of many dead pilots. In almost every case, I found a letter, *To be opened in the event of my death.* I am sure that they never admitted this foreboding among themselves. But it was there. Death had already become their companion when they were training and afterwards, flying with their squadrons. The experience of death was not new to them when the war began. It was merely intensified and made more horrible. This risk was the price they paid for being allowed to live with the clouds, the wind and the stars. They came to know the heavens better than they knew the earth. Pilots and gunners and navigators shared this privilege although they seldom spoke of it among themselves. They may have had a limited vocabulary, but the thoughts behind their pedestrian sentences were mighty and beautiful.

I think that the double risk of death, which was always with them, made them all the more grateful for life. Each time they landed they gave thanks. Perhaps it was in the form of a drink. They drank to celebrate, never to stimulate false ecstacy or to drown depression. They drank to celebrate. It was, and is, one of the most enchanting aspects of their talent for pleasure.

Life and death are not so very far apart from them. How many times I have seen a little group of bare-headed young pilots, so young that life was still a fresh gift in their hands, carrying a coffin into a church, or watching it being lowered into a dark hollow in the earth!

But there is no remorse, even when some form of fear remains. They do not necessarily conquer fear. They adapt themselves to it and beat it into a positive part of their character. For their fear and their sensibility are one.

The habits of the pilots show a frank, open-hearted acceptance of certain facts: that the price of double happiness must be paid for with the coin of double risk. So every living moment must be exhausted in joy. They resent idleness because it means waste of time from which pleasure might be wrung. This was true before the war, when the risks were those of peacetime flying. It is still true, with the added risks of war. It was true ten and even twenty years ago when the Air Force was numbered in thousands. The gaiety of pilots has always been that of men who were prepared to die at any moment, in return for the privilege of enjoying the beauty and danger of flight. They knew the terms of their bargain when they learned to fly and they were prepared to keep the bargain when the time came.

28

Peter Townsend and Dickie Lee had been posted to an aerodrome a few miles from the house … a secret place tucked away in the fields on the Suffolk border. In the early summer, John and I went out to find them. The people in the villages had already changed under the anxieties of war. I remember a haughty farmer's wife who refused to help us when we lost ourselves, wandering, down the lanes. Neither our uniforms nor our passes would warm her heart so we had to behave like Red Indians, finally espying the squadron of aircraft, lurking within the shelter of the trees. We found Peter and Dickie and took them back to the house. Dickie followed the car on a hellish motor bicycle. It was a pleasant enough afternoon and we lay on the lawn, the four of us, with a bowl of ice, a bottle of gin, some tonic water and four glasses, and talked the world away. All three looked older. Both Dickie and Peter had been shot down and a certain solemnity seemed to have touched them. Dickie had changed more than the others. We used to call him Dopey in the old days because he always fell asleep if the conversation took a serious turn. He was already a hero and in most of the newspapers there had been photographs of him receiving his decorations from the King. The long hell in France had left creases at the corner of his sleepy eyes. But he would have none of our attempts at war talk. He said that he had a date with a blonde in Saffron Walden and that he could not stay very long. Dickie's taste in blondes was not always reassuring to his friends, but he was obviously more concerned with his date than with our efforts to make him talk of how he had won the DFC and DSO on his tunic. I remember that when he stood up to go I noticed a hole in the leg of his trousers. It was where a bullet had gone through without touching his skin. I suppose that Peter and John and I were a bit pensive, being the older ones, so Dickie yawned and said, 'Well, I must get cracking.'

He made one gesture to sentiment before he went. On the day that war was declared he had left his favourite pictures with me ... before his squadron flew off to France. They were photographs of friends, of aircraft, and one of a spaniel. He asked me for them, so I brought them down from the attic and he flew off to his blonde with them, piled before him on the screeching, violent motor bicycle.

So Peter, John and I were alone. The war had hardened John. But Peter was tortured rather than exulted by his victories over the enemy and he was troubled as to what would come out of the war. I remember that he said, 'The only way a man can qualify for leadership is through personal example and thus parliament is condemned.' The sentence may sound a little sententious standing alone. But it grew naturally out of our argument over the world as we would like it to be when the war is ended. I asked him then, 'But you who survive the war must be the leaders of the peace. If you believe in what you are fighting for, then you should go into parliament when it is over and see that the right kind of world is built.' Then he sighed and answered, 'It would cost three thousand pounds to become a member of parliament and none of the pilots who are left will have three thousand pounds when the war ends.'

We talked then of the secret wish so many of us have to leave England when the war is over. Soldiers never revisit battlefields. There is something sad and repellent about the earth upon which one has fought for one's life. Pilots seem to feel this. They talk of farms in California and of indolent days on South Sea Islands. While the battle is on, they dream of escaping directly it is over. But when you remind them that their true duty is to their brothers who have been killed, then they agree and they know that they will stay. The Peters among them realise that with the declaration of peace their true work will begin.

29

John went back to 43 Squadron to take his part in a problem which beset many other squadrons about this time. 43 as he had known it almost came to an end on the evening when he sat on the edge of the aerodrome with George Lott, waiting for the rest of the squadron, who did not come back. Some were prisoners, maybe. Others might come back by the devious ways that were already operating across the Channel. New pilots had to be trained into the code of 43 and Flight-Lieutenant Tom Morgan was brought from the Air Ministry to take over B Flight, and Flying Officer Carey, who had been a Sergeant Pilot with the squadron in the first months of the war, also came back, with the experience of war in France to add to his usefulness.

There was one more disaster to harass the squadron before it resumed its place in the front line. One day while John was in London, George Lott and his section were ordered off from Tangmere, in very bad weather, to investigate some plots approaching the aerodrome from the south. Almost as soon as they broke cloud, they saw six Messerschmitt 110s flying away from them. The enemy had the advantage and they turned back and opened fire with their cannon. George was flying John's aircraft. A cannon shell hit the windscreen which splintered and filled George's right eye with glass. He was bleeding badly. The wound was so terrible that he eventually lost his eye. But he said nothing. He took refuge in cloud while the Germans were engaged by the other two. George called them up and told them to return to base. He was almost blinded then and his difficulties were increased by the clouds which hung close to the ground. At last, George found Arundel Castle. While flying at 500 feet, he had to abandon his aircraft.

John wrote to me two days later:

I have just been to see George (Group Captain Lott now commands a station in England) at Haslar Hospital. He is in terrible pain. They have operated to try and save his eye, but it has failed. Tonight they are taking his eye out. It will relieve the pain. His other eye will be OK.

Hector, I think I admire him as much as any human being I know. He began in the Service as an AC2. I think he's been in the RAF something like eighteen years. I remember you saying to me once something about the RAF being a school for character. The phrase was something like that. If ever a great character emerged from the RAF, it is George. God, I do admire his guts. I am sorry if I did not make it clear about Tony (Anthony Woods-Scawen, who had been shot down on the day when 43 Squadron suffered so severely while over France). George and I were having a lunchtime drink in the hall when Tony walked in, wearing an army shirt and a tin hat. Under his arm was his same old parachute. On the 7th, when we lost him, he had baled out over the German lines. He landed all right and hid in a ditch. After it was dark, he crept out and he walked twenty miles, still hanging on to his parachute. He found a British patrol with whom he was eventually evacuated.

But I wish you could have seen him walk into the mess, his face covered with smiles. He said to George, 'I am sorry I am late, sir.' All George did was to call Macey and say, 'Bring us a drink.' George asked Tony why he had lugged his parachute all the way home with him and Tony said, 'Well, I know that this one works and I might have to use it again'. He was shot down and saved by his parachute no less than six times. The seventh time he was shot down he was killed.

The new boys are doing fine. Tom Morgan is first rate. He shot down his first Hun yesterday – a Heinkel. There's a lot of activity now that the blitz has really begun. Caesar is out of hospital and on leave in Guildford. Carey and I are going up to London to have a party with him tonight.

30

Caesar Hull had brought a great story back from Norway, but when I saw him in London he talked of only the foolish part of it: the songs, the escapades and the parties when the battle was over.

He commanded a flight of Gladiators in the second expedition to Norway when we sent a squadron to fight the Luftwaffe on their stolen ground and to encourage and protect our own troops as they moved out under German pressure. It was a hopeless adventure; a gallant closing gesture before the last Nazi shadow fell on Norway.

Batchy Atcherley, my friend of Transjordan, was the Wing Commander who prepared the landing sites in Norway during the two weeks before the Gladiators arrived. There was no darkness when night came and he worked on with his men, day after day, until they had cut runways through the forest and built protecting bays for the aircraft with the fallen trees.

The Gladiators left on their second expedition in May of 1940, by aircraft carrier. At three o'clock in the morning of 20 May, the first of them took off for Badufoss, where Batchy and the ground crews were waiting for them. An hour or so afterwards the second section took off from the aircraft carrier, into terrible weather, led by a Swordfish from the Fleet Air Arm. There was heavy mist when they came to Senga Island and, through a slight error in navigation, it crashed into the side of a mountain. Some of the Gladiators rammed the slope in its wake.

But the section which Caesar was leading got through safely and they landed at Badufoss. Only sixteen Gladiators remained to carry on the campaign.

Batchy has since told me:

I had been at Badufoss for two weeks when Caesar and the others arrived. It was a filthy bad morning. Then those Gladiators plopped on to the ground and brought me back to normal. I had not known Caesar before, although I had heard many stories of his courage and of the days at Tangmere with 43. Caesar was a Hurricane in himself. He drank his life in quick gulps. He lacked all the textbook elements of leadership, yet he was a great leader, completely unconscious of the qualities that made him so. He was frightfully good company. Colossal dash. Bold in the air and a cracking good shot. He had every single qualification that a man could have. He was effervescent but never bubbly. He was able and bloody brave. I don't think there was anything lacking in him. His leadership was based on excellence in everything.

Batchy went on:

The climax of our show in Norway was at Bodo in the south. It was Caesar's show. I received a signal that our forces at Bodo needed air co-operation. I sent Caesar off, with two other pilots, knowing that there was nothing waiting for them in the way of a landing ground but a ploughed field and mud up to their knees. But we had to let the Tommies see a British aircraft and the job had to be done. Our army was retreating up a valley east of Bodo without any British aircraft to cover them. Caesar and the other two pilots landed in the muddy field and just as their wheels sank in, a Heinkel flew over them. However, they were not hit. Landing was one thing. Taking off from such mud was impossible. There was light during the night at that time of the year and Caesar and the others worked on, dragging boards from the walls of the huts and spreading them over the mud so that they would have a runway thirty or forty yards long, to take off from in the morning.

Caesar's own diary tells the rest of the story:

… the army were retreating up a valley east of Bodo and were being strafed by the Huns all day. Sounded too easy so I took off just as another Heinkel 111 circled the aerodrome. God! What a take-off! Came unstuck about fifty yards from the end and just staggered over the trees. Jack followed and crashed. I thought the expedition was doomed to failure and that I had better do as much damage as I could before landing again, so told Tony to land, over the blower, and set off towards the valley.

Saw some smoke rising, so investigated and found a Heinkel 111 at about 600 feet. Attacked it three times and it turned south with smoke pouring from fuselage and engines. Broke off attack to engage a Junkers 52 which crashed in flames. Saw Heinkel 111 flying south, tried to intercept and failed. Returned and attacked two Junker 52s in formation. Number one went into clouds. Number two crashed in flames after six people had baled out.

Attacked Heinkel 111 and drove it south with smoke pouring from it. Ammunition finished so returned to base.

The troops were very cheered by the report and I thought another patrol might produce some fun … This time the valley was deserted and the only thing I could do was amuse the troops by doing some aerobatics. They all cheered and waved madly every time I went down low – I think they imagined that at least we had air control and their worries were over.

Vain hope! Returned to base after two and a half hours. Everyone felt dead tired, so off we went to the RAF billet – a grand little house with every modern luxury, including some beer.

Caesar's performance that day was astonishing: four enemy aircraft brought down with one ammunition load. Next day, the two lonely Gladiators were sent off to cover the evacuation of 2,000 of our troops from Rognum. Caesar wrote:

… met Tony over the Salte Valley. It was a beautiful morning, but at Rognum the troops were blowing up ammunition and pushing off in larger 'puffers', as the flat-bottomed boats were called. One had a feeling of impending disaster as the evacuation looked so vulnerable, and we were a puny force to protect it against any vigorous onslaught. Tony and I did some formation and then we went off to refuel. I amused myself by shooting up the boats – and how those chaps waved! It did one good to see their pathetic confidence.

At eight o'clock that morning Caesar went into action again. He wrote:

Suddenly the balloon went up. There were 110s and 87s all around us, and the 87s started dive-bombing a jetty about 300 yards from the aerodrome. Tony's aircraft started at once and I waved him off. Then, after trying mine for a bit longer, got yellow and, together with the fitter, made a dive into a nearby barn. From there we watched the dive-bombing in terror until it seemed they were not actually concentrating on the aerodrome. Got the Gladiator going and shot off without helmet or waiting to do anything up. Circled the 'drome, climbing, and pinned an 87 at the bottom of its dive. It made off slowly over the sea and just as I was turning away, another 87 shot up past me and its shots went through my windscreen, knocking me out for a little while. Came to and was thanking my lucky stars when I heard a rat-tat behind me and felt my Gladiator hit. Went into a right-hand turn and dive, but could not get out of it. Had given up hope at 200 feet when she centralised and I gave her a burst of engine to clear some large rocks. Further rat-tats behind me so gave up hope and decided to get down. Held off, then crashed.

Caesar had been wounded in his head and in one knee. He crawled on his stomach through the deep mud, with the battle still being fought above him. When he was found he was taken to hospital.

Batchy Atcherley told me the rest of the story. Caesar was lying in hospital with his leg in plaster. In the next bed was a man who was convinced that he was dying.

'That chap is dying in rather a noisy way. Don't you think you could do something about it?' said Caesar. The Germans intervened. Next morning they dropped a stick of bombs across the hospital. Caesar leapt from his bed, hacked the plaster from his leg and jumped through the window. But the dying man leapt through the window line abreast and passed Caesar in the first 50 yards.

Batchy sent Caesar home to England in a Sunderland and he was ill for some time. But he recovered before the Battle of Britain in which he fought and was killed.

31

John's squadron were soon re-formed and back in the battle. Two weeks passed between the time of his leave and the day when he was to appear at Buckingham Palace to receive his DFC and in this time he brought down two more Messerschmitts, both on the same day. But his new glory ended rather sadly ... he crashed into a villa at Worthing and landed in a cucumber frame, with a broken collarbone.

I travelled to the South Coast in the late afternoon of the following day and found him propped up, with nurses to fuss over him and a view of the sea. By this time I was playing Tacitus to his Agricola so I sat down and wrote his story, as he told it to me:

It was a lovely evening and the wind was warm about us as we passed through the slipstream of our aircraft to our cockpits. We were to patrol the coast at 10,000 feet and we soon reached the patrol line at this height. I could see for miles. There was a thin layer of cloud one thousand feet above us and it shaded our eyes from the sun.

We were flying east when three enemy aircraft were seen flying west in the clouds overhead. I told my leader that I would climb above the clouds with my flight and investigate. As I did this, no less than twelve Messerschmitt 109 fighters emerged from the clouds. Still climbing, I made for the sun and turned and gave the order for my flight to break up and attack. In a moment our battle began. Our six Hurricanes were against the enemy's twelve.

The eighteen aircraft chased round and round in and out of the cloud. I chose my first opponent. He seemed to be dreaming and I quickly got on to his tail and gave him a short burst which damaged him. I flew in closer and gave him a second dose. It was enough. He dived, out of control, and I followed him down to 6,000 feet. There I circled for a minute or two and watched him dive vertically into the calm sea. There was only the telltale patch of oil on the water to mark where he had disappeared.

I opened my hood for a breath of fresh air and looked about the sky. There was no sign of either the enemy or of my own flight. I was alone, so I climbed back into the cloud which was thin and misty. Three Messerschmitts, flying in line astern, crossed in front of me, so close that I could see the black crosses on their wings and fuselages. I opened fire on number three of the formation. We went round and round, in decreasing circles, as I fired. I was lucky again. I had the pleasure of seeing my bullets hit him. Pieces of his wings flew off and black smoke came from just behind his cockpit. He dived and I fired one more burst at him, directly from astern. We were doing a phenomenal speed. Then my ammunition gave out just as the other two Messerschmitts attacked me. The cloud was too thin to be of help. It was merely misty and you could see the blue of the sky throughout. So I had to rely on my aeroplane. I twisted and turned and dived towards the coast. I was flying at about 16,000 feet, eight miles or so out to sea. But they were too accurate. I could hear the deafening thud of their bullets hitting the armour plate behind my back and I could see great hunks being torn off my wings. There was a strong smell of glycol in the cockpit, so I knew that the radiator had been hit. What little wisps of cloud there were, were far beyond my reach and my engine was chugging badly. It was terribly hot.

Then came a cold stinging pain in my left foot. One of the Jerry bullets had found its mark. But it really did not hurt much. I tried to dive faster to the sea and make my escape, low down, when the control column became useless in my hand. Black smoke poured into the cockpit and I could not see.

I knew that I must leave the aircraft.

Everything after this was perfectly calm. I was now at about 10,000 feet, but still some miles out to sea. I lifted my seat, undid my harness and opened the hood. The wind was my ally. It felt like a hand lifting me from the cockpit, by my hair. But it was actually a combination of the wind and the slipstream catching under my helmet and pulling me free of the aircraft. It was a pleasant sensation. I found myself in midair, beautifully cool and dropping without any feeling of speed. It seemed hours before I reminded myself to pull my ripcord and open my parachute. This part was quite easy. The noise of the wind stopped and there was a terrific jerk. It seemed that my body was being pulled in every place at the same time. Then I began to swing like a pendulum. Then I vomited, just as I looked down and saw the coast and the sea near Worthing.

I stopped swinging and settled down to look about me. Then I had a horrible fear. I felt terribly afraid of falling out of my harness into the sea. I put my hands up and held the straps above me. I was frightened of touching the quick release box on my tummy by mistake.

I became calm and I was able to enjoy the full view of the world below. The beach was some miles away, with soldiers. And there were the long lines of villas in Worthing. There was no sensation of speed. I knew I was descending only because the ripples on the water became bigger and the soldiers on the beach seemed to grow.

Then came a minute of anxiety. As I floated down one of the Messerschmitts appeared. The pilot circled around me and I was alarmed. He was near enough for me to see his face … as much as I could see with his helmet and goggles. I felt very much that he would shoot me. And I felt helpless. But he didn't shoot. He behaved very well. He flew so near the noise of his aircraft was terrific. He flew around me about one and a half times and then he suddenly opened a piece of his hood and waved to me. Then he dived towards the sea and made off across the Channel to France.

I'd like to know why he let me get away. He could have got me as simply as anything. But he didn't try.

When I recovered from my fear I found that the wind was still being friendly. It was carrying me in towards the beach. I took out my cigarettes and lit one with my lighter without any difficulty. Ages seemed to pass and I was quite happy. I had forgotten about my foot but I suppose that it had been bleeding all the time because I began to feel rather sleepy. I threw away my cigarette as I came nearer and nearer to the beach. I heard the 'All Clear' siren and as I passed over the beach and the houses on the sea front, I could see people coming out of their shelters – people looking up at me. I was then at about 1,000 feet.

The changing temperature of the air at a low level seemed to affect my speed and I began to sway a little. I could hear my parachute flapping like the sound of a sail in a small boat. The soldiers' faces became quite clear. I could see their rifles but they were not pointing at me. I must have looked English, even at a thousand feet. This was comforting.

I became anxious again, for the first time since the enemy pilot circled around me. I was afraid that my escapade was to end by my being killed against the wall of a seaside villa. It did not seem possible that I could reach the fields beyond. It was all very quick after that. I seemed to rush … and then I hit the roof, or the edge of the roof, of a house. I suppose my parachute crumpled then because the next thing I realised was that I was going through a garden fence backwards, and then, bang into a cucumber frame.

I lay still for a moment. Then I released my parachute. I don't know quite what happened. I was in pain. My collarbone was broken and I was pretty badly bruised from hitting the house and the fence. And my foot was still bleeding. But I remember that when I released my parachute and lay still, my brain was quite clear, and I whimpered because I was so grateful for being alive.

It was a little house and a little garden. The woman ran out and others came, because they had seen me coming down I suppose. The woman brought me tea and then a policeman came with a glass of whisky. He was in the street and he handed it over the garden wall. I drank the whisky and then the tea. There seemed to be about twenty people wanting to be kind to me. The woman who owned the garden brought me a blanket. My ankle and shoulder were bound up and an ambulance arrived …

I was in awful pain, but my mind was quite clear. I remember that as I was being lifted into the ambulance, there were some men who had seen the battle and they seemed to know that I had brought down a Hun. One of them said, 'we saw what you did, sir,' and then a woman pushed a little boy forward and said, 'Ernie, give the gentleman those cigarettes.' And the little boy came running up to me and said, 'Good luck, sir. When I grow up I'm going to be an airman too!'

32

In the summer of 1919, the present King flew over Windsor Castle on his first cross-country flight of 80 miles. His father's stubborn distrust of flying had been broken down and he had been allowed to become a pilot. His instructor had said of him, 'He had the rare quality which an instructor always dreams of instilling into his pupil. By instinct he was able to use eyes hands and brain in unison.'

Twenty-three years have passed since then and many people have forgotten that the King is a qualified pilot. But pilots in the Royal Air Force remember that the wings he wears are not merely an ornament upon his tunic. It is a source of satisfaction for them that their honours for achievement in the air come from a sovereign who is himself a pilot. The duties of kingship may have anchored King George VI to the earth but he knows a little of the skies to which the pilots belong and there is therefore a very real bond between them when they stand before him, to accept decorations from his hand.

33

The courtyard of Buckingham Palace, where John was given his Distinguished Flying Cross, has since been bombed. But on the morning in August when his mother, his sister Ruth and I walked under the stone arch there was only one hint of war. An amiable silver balloon hovered overhead, against a pure summer sky. There were lazy pigeons looking down at us from the cornices and white butterflies fluttering over the wives and mothers and brothers of the heroic company. They were there because Queen Elizabeth had said, 'I think they should come. If my husband were receiving a decoration, I'd like to be there to see him.'

The scene was very simple. There were no flags. There was a rather sprightly band in the background playing lilting tunes and marches. The canopy of London summer was spread over us. The first of the procession was a soldier who received the Victoria Cross from the King. Then came a sailor who bent low beneath his sovereign's sword to be knighted. Then came an Air Marshal and a white-haired old Admiral who must have seen half a century of wars.

The King received the procession of heroes, with serenity and stillness. The line of soldiers, sailors and pilots was long. John was almost at the end. His arm was still in a sling. At last he climbed the dais and stood before the King.

There is only one source of honour in the land. I saw the King fix the DFC on John's tunic. For me it meant that a diffident boy, who had confessed weakness and little else six years before, had played his part in the resurrection of his country. His armament had been courage, modesty and goodness of heart.

34

One more adventure was waiting for John before he was allowed to rest. A few days after he received his DFC from the King he went to Tangmere to collect his car and some clothes for his convalescence. As he drove from Chichester to Tangmere the sirens sounded. Some Ju 87s and some Dorniers, flying high and surrounded by fighters, had been spotted approaching the coast of Sussex.

John drove on to the aerodrome and as he passed the married quarters, he saw scores of aircraft overhead. The first bomb fell and he threw himself into a ditch. He wrote later of the raid:

The noise was terrific. I could hear it, although I had my hands tightly over my ears and my head well down in the ditch. The bombs dropped all around me and I was terrified. I looked up now and then, but not very often. I saw black smoke. The smell of cordite and dust was horrible. I couldn't see much ... I only saw two Ju 87s drop their bombs from my ditch. Each bomb shook the earth and gave my shoulder hell.

The raid did not last long. But it was long enough. There were more than 240 enemy aircraft in the whole raid that day, but some of them had gone off to bomb Portsmouth and Southampton.

When the three minutes had passed, there was sudden silence. All I could hear was the crackling of a burning building, and a fire-tender that drove past me at a hellish speed. I got up slowly. Two airmen got out of a slit trench a few yards away and asked me if I was all right. They were as dazed as I was. I was all right, but I realised that with my ankle and arm I would not be of much use. The smoke and flames and dust forced me into my car, which was dented where a piece of shrapnel had struck it. I drove off to Arundel to lunch.

I came back soon afterwards feeling better, but rather nervous. It was pretty horrible seeing Tangmere, which I have always loved so much, badly pasted by bombs. Bricks and piles of broken glass blocked the way to the mess and there was an endless tangle of

1. Peter Townsend and Caesar Hull. Caesar shot down four German aircraft on one mission in Norway in an antiquated Gladiator biplane.

2. Laurie Lorimer and George Feeny.

3. Members of 43 Squadron photographed in the North of Scotland. Left to right: Sergeant Buck, Pilot Officer Tony Woods-Scawen who was shot down and saved by the same parachute six times. Asked why he carried his parachute 20 miles across France he'd said 'well, I know this one works'. Flight Lieutenant Caesar Hull, Flying Officer Wilkinson, Sergeant Garton.

4. Larch trees cut down by John Simpson's aircraft when it crashed on 21 February 1940.

5. Fitters and riggers carrying out an inspection on John Simpson's Hurricane. John's rigger: 'The most interesting time is when they come back from action. We all clamour round. There are bags of excitement when our pilots have brought some Jerries down. And then you look for bulletholes, because you become sort of attached to your own kite. I suppose it's like a groom with a horse.'

6. Armourers re-arming John Simpson's Hurricane.

Top: 7. John Simpson briefing pilots of his squadron in Northern Ireland.
Left: 8. Dickie Lee.

Top: 9. Kitson (centre) with two friends,
before he joined his squadron.
Right: 10. George Lott.

Top: 11. 43 Squadron. John Simpson is fourth from the left.
Left: 12. Blenheims over south east England, 1940. John's squadron had a 'pool' Blenheim which he flew to Blackpool for a few days leave with MacEwen on 3 February 1940.

13. Readiness.

Opposite: 14. Ground crew rearming Hurricanes. John's Rigger again: 'You know, when Operations tell us to take cover we take our rifles with us and go to the dugout. Well, this day, the Dornier came well within rifle range and my mate and I got in ten rounds apiece. I hope we hit him. The Hurricanes brought it down, but I felt that I was a bit of an ace after that.' From the Battle of Britain Monument (Victoria embankment, London) sculptured by Paul Day.

Top: 15. Ground staff overhauling the Rolls Royce Merlin engine in the Hurricane.
Above: 16. Hurricanes being refuelled immediately on return to their base.

17. Women at work in fighter aircraft production. Battle of Britain veteran Tom Neil: 'By the end of a day we could have five serviceable aircraft out of 18, but by noon the next day we were back to full strength. We didn't know where they came from – they just did and that was the wonderful thing about our supply system.' It was often women who also ferried the newly built aircraft direct to fighter airfields, members of the Air Transport Auxiliary (ATA). From the Battle of Britain Monument (Victoria embankment, London) sculptured by Paul Day.

18. An aircraft spotter of the Observer Corps on the roof of a building in London on the look out for enemy aircraft, 1940. St Paul's Cathedral is in the background.

Top: 19. Observer Corps on the look out for enemy aircraft. After radar they were the second line of defense. From the Battle of Britain Monument (Victoria embankment, London) sculptured by Paul Day.

Right: 20. Operations Room. It was from here that John Simpson would be directed towards enemy aircraft via his R/T.

21. An air battle is in progress. In the Operations Room of a fighter station Plotters with their croupier-like sticks mark up the position of the aircraft, while others man operational telephones. John: 'I spoke to George Knox who was controlling and told him of my success. I could hear over the R/T he and the whole Ops room seemed to go mad. You see, it meant a lot to them for it was their first victory (the squadron were lodgers on a Coastal Command Station. A fighter victory was unique on a station whose combats were all with submarines far out in the Atlantic). George said he had seen the Hun's track suddenly disappear off the map in the Control Room. He said 'It's too good to be true.' He asked me all about it over the R/T, which was rather naughty. And he said there would be a party for me when I landed'.

22. A plotter takes tally cards to mark up the position of squadrons on the indicator board.

23. In the Control Room of a fighter station R/T operators keep contact with pilots. One operator marks up the position of a fighter on the indicator board, while others give pilots instructions to land.

24. A view of the operations room showing plotters at work on the table, a wartime image issued to the press with the actual plotting map obliterated for security reasons.

25. Three fighter pilots live in a caravan beside their aircraft ready for instant action.

26. Fighter pilots pass the time waiting for action 1940.

27. A typical scene in a dispersal hut showing members of a fighter squadron waiting for the call for action, 1940.

28. Fighter pilots play ha'penny while they wait for the call to 'scramble', 1940.

30. Pilots scramble to their Spitfires, June 1940.

31. A fighter pilot springs into action when the order comes, 1940.

Opposite: 29. 'Scramble'. From the alert relayed from a fighter station to the airfields fighters could be in the air within minutes. From the Battle of Britain Monument (Victoria embankment, London) sculptured by Paul Day.

32. A Hawker Hurricane 8-gun fighter as flown by John Simpson.

33. Formations of Hurricanes, 1940. John Simpson didn't take to flying in formation very quickly.

34. Spitfire returning from a combat mission, August 1940. John Simpson tried the Spitfire but preferred Hurricanes.

35. Spitfire in flight, 1940.

36. Spitfires on patrol, 1940.

37. Hurricanes pulling away after making contact with German aircraft.

38. Formations of Hurricanes, 1940.

39. A Ju 87 'Stuka' dive bomber. John Simpson saw them in action over Dunkirk:
'...And wrecked ships on the beach: wrecked ships of all sizes, sticking out of the water. And
a destroyer cut in halves by a bomb. I saw it! A Junkers 87 came low over the water and
seemed to fly into the destroyer and drop its bomb. That was pretty terrible. It was shot
down after, thank God. I saw the destroyer crack in two. And I saw parachutes coming down
from wrecked aircraft, landing in the water and on the beach and on the land'.

40. An Me 110. John Simpson's fourth 'kill' which he shot down over Dunkirk: 'I climbed up again and found that more German fighters, Messerschmitt 110s, also strangers to us, had joined in. I got on to the tail of one of them, which was firing at a Hurricane piloted by Crackers. I got so close that when I fired, his tail just blew off in mid-air'.

41. An Me 109 in flight. An 109 was John Simpson's third 'kill' (and first fighter) over Dunkirk: 'After avoiding several on my tail, for what seemed to be ages, I got on to one and opened fire. We chased about and lost height rapidly, coming down to 5,000 feet above the land. When he was diving I got in a steady burst and he crumbled up as if he were made of cardboard. He crashed in flames on a golf course'.

Top: 42. John Simpson's second 'kill' was a Dornier 17 on 9 May 1940. 'I blew his nose right off. I must have killed the pilot. It burned furiously and dived into the sea and exploded. A terrible but a wonderful sight. Three people had jumped out of the rear gun position and I saw them fall from about 800 feet into the sea. I could not see the aircraft after it crashed into the water. Only a column of fire and black smoke. I saw one of the Germans in the water. I noted my position and flew back to base'. From the Battle of Britain Monument (Victoria embankment, London) sculptured by Paul Day.

Right: 43. A Ju 88. John's tenth 'kill' was a Ju 88.

Top and below: 45. & 46. Air combat, a Spitfire pilot trying to avoid cannon shells fired from an Me 109 on his tail. From the Battle of Britain Monument (Victoria embankment, London) sculptured by Paul Day.

Opposite: 44. A Hurricane attacking an Me 109. From the Battle of Britain Monument (Victoria embankment, London) sculptured by Paul Day.

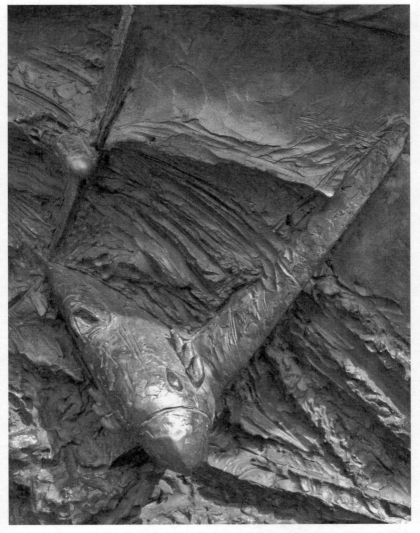

48. Air combat, a Spitfire pilot trying to avoid cannon shells fired from an Me 109 on his tail. From the Battle of Britain Monument (Victoria embankment, London) sculptured by Paul Day.

Opposite: 47. A fighter pilot with R/T equipment. From the Battle of Britain Monument (Victoria embankment, London) sculptured by Paul Day.

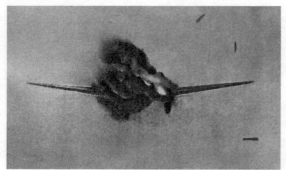

49, 50. & 51. British gun-camera images of German aircraft being shot down.

'I singled out a Messerschmitt 109 and had a very exciting combat with him. He was a good pilot and he hit me several times. We began to do aerobatics and while he was on his back, I got in a burst which set him on fire. He jumped out, but I did not see his parachute open. His machine was almost burned out before it hit the ground. There were scores of fighters about me, but I still had plenty of ammunition. I got on to the tail of another 109 and while I was firing at him two Messerschmitt 110s fired at me from either side. I continued to fire at the 109 which was badly winged. He suddenly stall turned sharply to the right, went into a spin and crashed straight into one of the other Messerschmitts which was firing at me.

I couldn't resist following them down. It was a wonderful sight. They stuck together in a sort of embrace of flames, until they were a few hundred feet above the ground. Then they parted and crashed, less than twenty yards apart.'

Above: 52. The Battle of Britain was very visible to the British from the ground with swirling vapour trails marking the dogfights in the summer skies of 1940.

Below: 53. A doomed German Dornier 17 bomber aircraft plummeting earthwards after being attacked by British fighters.

54. A downed Me 109. This was the Luftwaffe's main fighter.

55. A downed He 111. John Simpson's first 'kill' was a Heinkel 111e on 13 February 1940. 'I hit him fair and square in the wings and fuselage. One of his engines stopped and bits of metal flew off. He then disappeared into some wisps of cloud … I caught up and finished all my ammunition on him. He was burning well when he disappeared into the mist above the sea'.

56. A downed Dornier 17, August 1940.

In September 1940 John & Hector saw several German bombers come down near Hector's house in Essex: 'A German bomber was hurtling down from the sky, with a scarf of smoke at its tail. It dived into a distant field. We heard the explosion as it hit the ground. Then we looked up. High in the sky, four parachutes were floating down … lovely, flower-like parachutes, with men swinging to and fro beneath them. The sound of machine-gun bullets guided our eyes. Over our heads were two formations of bombers surrrounded by fighters … the fighters darting backwards and forwards so that it was not easy to know if they were ours or theirs. The bombers moved towards the aerodrome and then we heard the thud of the bombs. Debden was getting it. Then another bomber was flung out of the pattern above us … flung so that it crashed into a thousand pieces. Then a third fell and the flaming pieces of fuselage made a dangerous rain over the garden. All six of the enemy came down … before they could recross the coast. Two of ours limped out of the battle and crashed among the distant trees. We went into the fields to watch the parachutes slowly descending. Then we jumped into the car and sped down the narrow Essex lanes. The hedges bristled with guns. It was strange how the whole countryside had suddenly awakened … the sleepy acres of farmland became belligerent. We left the car and ran through clover with the old farmers, to wait for the Germans to land. In one hollow we came upon a burning Messerschmitt. I shall never forget the fierce core of the flame. There was no vestige of the crew. John and I followed an old farmer we knew. He had seen a German land … the fluttering parachute settling slowly into the stubble. He was a few yards ahead of us, so we left him to his victory. He peeped through the hedge, to be certain first that his prisoner was not holding a grenade. Centuries of peace had not dulled the edge of his valour or his caution. He was a fine old man, with a beard and quick eyes. He climbed through the hedge and captured his man'.

57. A Dornier 17 after having crash-landed, 1940.

Above left: 59. 'Down in the drink'. A pilot who bailed out over the Channel is rescued by an air/sea rescue launch.
Above right: 60. A Hurricane coming in to refuel and re-arm. A photograph taken during the Battle of Britain.
Below: 61. A Hurricane fighter pilot having returned from a combat mission, 1940.

Opposite top left: 58. An RAF pilot bailing out. John parachuted out of his Hurricane after first shooting down two Me 109s on 19 July 1940: 'Everything after this was perfectly calm. I was now at about 10,000 feet, but still some miles out to sea. I lifted my seat, undid my harness and opened the hood. The wind was my ally. It felt like a hand lifting me from the cockpit, by my hair. But it was actually a combination of the wind and the slipstream catching under my helmet and pulling me free of the aircraft. It was a pleasant sensation. I found myself in midair, beautifully cool and dropping without any feeling of speed. It seemed hours before I reminded myself to pull my ripcord and open my parachute. This part was quite easy. The noise of the wind stopped and there was a terrific jerk. It seemed that my body was being pulled in every place at the same time. Then I began to swing like a pendulum. Then I vomited, just as I looked down and saw the coast and the sea near Worthing.

I stopped swinging and settled down to look about me. Then I had a horrible fear. I felt terribly afraid of falling out of my harness into the sea. I put my hands up and held the straps above me. I was frightened of touching the quick release box on my tummy by mistake.

I became calm and I was able to enjoy the full view of the world below. The beach was some miles away, with soldiers. And there were the long lines of villas in Worthing. There was no sensation of speed. I knew I was descending only because the ripples on the water became bigger and the soldiers on the beach seemed to grow.

Then came a minute of anxiety. As I floated down one of the Messerschmitts appeared. The pilot circled around me and I was alarmed. He was near enough for me to see his face … as much as I could see with his helmet and goggles. I felt very much that he would shoot me. And I felt helpless. But he didn't shoot. He behaved very well. He flew so near the noise of his aircraft was terrific. He flew around me about one and a half times and then he suddenly opened a piece of his hood and waved to me. Then he dived towards the sea and made off across the Channel to France.

I'd like to know why he let me get away. He could have got me as simply as anything. But he didn't try.

When I recovered from my fear I found that the wind was still being friendly. It was carrying me in towards the beach. I took out my cigarettes and lit one with my lighter without any difficulty. Ages seemed to pass and I was quite happy. I had forgotten about my foot but I suppose that it had been bleeding all the time because I began to feel rather sleepy. I threw away my cigarette as I came nearer and nearer to the beach. I heard the 'All Clear' siren and as I passed over the beach and the houses on the sea front, I could see people coming out of their shelters – people looking up at me. I was then at about 1,000 feet.

The changing temperature of the air at a low level seemed to affect my speed and I began to sway a little. I could hear my parachute flapping like the sound of a sail in a small boat. The soldiers' faces became quite clear. I could see their rifles but they were not pointing at me. I must have looked English, even at a thousand feet. This was comforting.

I became anxious again, for the first time since the enemy pilot circled around me. I was afraid that my escapade was to end by my being killed against the wall of a seaside villa. It did not seem possible that I could reach the fields beyond. It was all very quick after that. I seemed to rush … and then I hit the roof, or the edge of the roof, of a house. I suppose my parachute crumpled then because the next thing I realised was that I was going through a garden fence backwards, and then, bang into a cucumber frame.

I lay still for a moment. Then I released my parachute. I don't know quite what happened. I was in pain. My collarbone was broken and I was pretty badly bruised from hitting the house and the fence. And my foot was still bleeding. But I remember that when I released my parachute and lay still, my brain was quite clear, and I whimpered because I was so grateful for being alive.

It was a little house and a little garden. The woman ran out and others came, because they had seen me coming down I suppose. The woman brought me tea and then a policeman came with a glass of whisky. He was in the street and he handed it over the garden wall. I drank the whisky and then the tea. There seemed to be about twenty people wanting to be kind to me. The woman who owned the garden brought me a blanket. My ankle and shoulder were bound up and an ambulance arrived …

I was in awful pain, but my mind was quite clear. I remember that as I was being lifted into the ambulance, there were some men who had seen the battle and they seemed to know that I had brought down a Hun. One of them said, 'we saw what you did, sir,' and then a woman pushed a little boy forward and said, 'Ernie, give the gentleman those cigarettes.' And the little boy came running up to me and said, 'Good luck, sir. When I grow up I'm going to be an airman too!'

62. A fighter pilot in full flying gear on the wing of his Hurricane.

63. On return to base pilots would be debriefed by the squadron intelligence officer who would complete a 'combat report' including details on any 'kills'.

Form "F"

IIV41(e13/1

PERSONAL **COMBAT REPORT**

Sector Serial No. _____ (A) N.E. 1.

Serial No. of Order detailing Flight or Squadron to
    Patrol _____ (B) _____

Date _____ (C) 13/5/41

Flight, Squadron _____ (D) Flight ~~O.~~ Sqdn. 245.

Number of Enemy Aircraft _____ (E) 1

Type of Enemy Aircraft _____ (F) Do. 17.

Time Attack was delivered _____ (G) 17.23.

Place Attack was delivered _____ (H) Approx 15 miles N.W. Stranraer.

Height of Enemy _____ (J) 0 feet

Enemy Casualties _____ (K) 1

Our Casualties _____ Aircraft _____ (L) Nil

    Personnel _____ (M) Nil

GENERAL REPORT _____ (R) _____

I was on my way to Ayr to
collect spares when I sighted an a/c
flying north very near the water, I thought
it odd for an a/c to be flying so low
in that direction so I gave chase and
after several minutes identified it as
a Do 17 using full boost I overtook
~~the~~ E/a at sea level & doing a stall
turn after climbing delivered a head on
diving attack. I do not think I hit the
e/a in this attack, as he started to
climb I did a beam attack from

Signature

O.C. { Section
       Flight:
       Squadron   Squadron No.

Above and opposite top: 64. John Simpson's combat report (from which the original
1943 edition of this book took its name) for his shooting down of his thirteenth
'kill', a Dornier 17. See pages 198–201.

the starboard quarter and saw my de Wilde bursting on his engines and fuselage. his starboard engine stopped during this attack, and I received return fire from a side M.G. The E/A was then now going very slowly & trying to turn (presumably towards land) I got in another burst from dead ahead & the e/a hit the water and overturned floating on its back for approx 3 mins then sinking nose first. I saw no one come out of the a/c, & consider the force of the impact knocked them out.

J.W. Simpson s/l

Below: 65. Nurses look after wounded RAF officers on the terrace of a hospital. Battle of Britain veteran Tom Neil: 'Our killing fields were roughly over the central part of Kent. Everyone in the squadron was shot down at one time or another. We got to know the hospitals in Kent like the backs of our hands'.

Top & opposite top: 66. & 68. The Dornier 17 'Flying Pencil', the most frequently encountered German bomber during the Battle of Britain. From the Battle of Britain Monument (Victoria embankment, London) sculptured by Paul Day.

Left: 67. Anti-aircraft gunners firing on German raiders above. From the Battle of Britain Monument (Victoria embankment, London) sculptured by Paul Day.

Below: 69. St Pauls through the smoke of the great fire raid of Sunday 29 December 1940.

70. Firemen of the London Auxiliary Fire Fighting Services during the Blitz, 1940.

Opposite bottom & this page: 71, 72. & 73. John Simpson and his fellow pilots were very conscious of the human cost of the blitz. John, on shooting down his eleventh 'kill', a fully laden He 111 bomber: 'Then I saw a comforting red glow in his belly. Below the glow was hanging an immense object. I could see the silhouette of it. I suppose it must have been a very heavy bomb or a mine and I think I must have hit it. I was still firing when the Heinkel blew up, with a terrific explosion which blew me upwards and sideways. I found out afterwards that bits of metal from the Hun had hit my left wing and had made a tear in the fuselage by the tail plane. When I righted myself, I was delighted to see showers of flaming pieces, like confetti on fire. We were now over the sea and I could see the little flaming bits falling through the cloud below me. I had travelled twenty or thirty miles during the combat. I was a bit shaken, but when my mind was quiet again I was able to enjoy the satisfaction of knowing that I had brought the bastard down before he had dropped his bombs on Belfast. Curious feeling of pleasure in this'.

Top: 75. A classic photograph of Hurricane pilots taken at the height of the Battle of Britain in July 1940.
Above: 76. One of the iconic images created by the Air Ministry of a Battle of Britain fighter pilot.
Opposite: 74. Winston Churchill surveys the Blitz-damaged House of Commons.

77. Cover of the 1941 Ministry of Information propaganda booklet which was the first book to lionise the 'Few'. It sold in the 100,000s.

78. 43 Squadron emblem. From the Battle of Britain Monument (Victoria embankment, London) sculptured by Paul Day.

79. John W. C. Simpson's name on the Battle of Britain monument on Victoria embankment in London.

wire and hose pipes. The hangar in which I used to keep my aircraft for repairs was burned out. It all looked pretty terrible.

I left the car and walked to the mess. Sitting on the table in the hall was Jack Boret, the Station Commander, dusty and dirty and with dry blood on his cheek. Some of the other officers were with him. All he said was, 'Hullo! You've arrived at a nice time. How are you?'

He said that there were not many casualties but that the damage was pretty bad. The sick quarters had gone – the armoury and half the big hangar in which we used to keep our cars. There were no windows left.

But the aerodrome was serviceable again in about eight hours. That is what really makes me wonder if these raids are worth the enemy's while. 43 Squadron was already in the air when the Huns arrived and the Station Commander told me that they had already got eleven confirmed that day.

He told me that Billy Fiske had crashed and that he was badly burned while flying with 601. Billy Fiske died that evening. He was the first United States pilot to lose his life in the war.

I had a drink with him and the others and then I went to see my room. There was a big hole in the wall and the plaster from the ceiling was all over the floor. The glass from the windows had all fallen rather curiously into one heap on the bed. I looked through the broken window frames and saw thirty yards away, where the new sick quarters used to stand, nothing but a heap of rubble. But there were very few people there when it happened. The smell made me feel sick so I threw a few things into a bag. I could not wait any longer, so I asked the Station Commander to give my love to 43 and I drove away.

35

In the first year of the war, 43 Squadron lost thirty-six pilots for the reward of ninety-seven German aircraft. Tubby Badger (Squadron Leader V. C. W. Badger, DFC, died a year later), who had been with 43 in the early days, came back as its third commanding officer since the war began. He was shot down on 30 August and was unable to fly again. Caesar Hull took over the command on 1 September, a fulfilment to his career which meant more to him than all his victories. He didn't live long enough to have the third stripe sewn on his sleeve. He led 43 through a succession of combats for only seven days. On 8 September he was found dead, beside his aircraft, in a field in Kent. He had been killed by a bullet during the Battle of the London Docks. The Huns had come over in continuous waves all day, and Caesar had led the squadron in to attack a formation of Dornier bombers. He was never seen alive again.

All the key men fighting with 43 were shot down or killed within eight days. Tubby Badger was shot down on 30 August. Tony Woods-Scawen was killed on 2 September (Flying Officer A. Woods-Scawen crashed near an aircraft of 85 Squadron which had also been shot down, in the same battle. Unknown to Tony Woods-Scawen, the aircraft was flown by his brother. They were killed within a few minutes of each other and fell side by side). Tom Morgan was shot down on 6 September and Caesar Hull and Dickie Reynell on 8 September. Dickie Reynell, one of the finest pilots in the country, was a Hawker Test Pilot and he had been attached to 43 for only two weeks to gain combat experience with a Hurricane.

The ranks of 43 were sadly thin when the squadron was posted to Usworth, on 9 September, to recover itself and reform for fresh battles.

John was resting his ankle and shoulder in Cornwall during the battles of August and September. He wrote to me on 4 September:

For two days I have been thinking of Caesar. I loved him as I would a brother. He was more than a rare person in the RAF, and there can never be anyone to replace him in character, charm and kindliness. We came to 43 together and grew up in it together. We knew each other from A to Z and it was a privilege no one else could share.

This hell cannot go on for ever. And reassure yourself with the feeling and knowledge that we do the same to them. I was glad I was here, in a quiet, calm place when the news came. I swim and fish with the wonderful old fishermen, and I walk miles into the woods every day. They are full of giant hydrangeas and wild orchids.

I had a wonderful letter from Mummy. My God, her courage is astounding.

I go down to the Sloop at St Ives for my glass of beer. The fishermen are there and some of them saw me in my uniform on the day I arrived. They are so grateful to the RAF it is frightening. Their stories of the sea and of their own courage, which they tell without realising what they are saying, put any bravery I thought I had in the shade. They make me feel very humble.

I have received my golden caterpillar for the parachute jump.

It is very pretty and it has two rubies for eyes. I am looking forward to wearing my uniform again so that I can show it off.

Your letter about Caesar. I don't know what to say. I thought I was quite used by now to people dying. Do you realise that there are only three of us who were with the squadron when the war began … still alive and serving with the squadron? But Caesar was like a brother. I went for a long walk in the woods when the news came and I cried for the first time since I was little.

Poor 43. But we can take it. We will have to begin all over again. New CO new pilots. But the squadron spirit is safe. Dear old Caesar. He commanded the squadron he began in as a pilot officer. I would have loved to fly with him as my CO.

It seems funny to think that I shall never see him shaking that left foot of his as he used to do when he was excited. And how he used to rub his nose between his thumb and forefinger when he was nervous. And that laugh!

He had a good life and I think that he loved every minute of it. I never heard anybody say an unkind thing about Caesar and I never heard him say an unkind thing about anybody else. One can't say more than that, can one?

36

The countryside seemed very empty when John and I snatched three-days of leave in Essex, before he went back to his squadron. There was nobody we knew at Duxford or at Debden. The Battle of Britain had taken still more of our friends. Rodney Wilkinson, with whom I used to drink bitter coffee in Jerusalem and who shared a house with me in London for a few months at the beginning of the war, had been killed almost as soon as he went back to operational flying. He was one of my oldest flying friends and when he was at Duxford, long before the war, he used to come to see John and myself and go into huddles of pilot talk. Once when he stayed for the weekend, he left at crack of dawn with my shaving brush. He flew over the house an hour after and dropped the brush, tied to a multi-coloured message streamer. Somebody in the village reported us to the police and the story grew into a scandal. My name ended with a vowel, so I was obviously Italian. And the aircraft that flew low over my house was obviously dropping messages from Mussolini.

And Kenneth Ferguson was killed. One summer afternoon he flew me over the Dead Sea, so low over the ancient water that the blossoms on the oleander bushes met me at eye level. Kenneth's prayers were the essence of his life and he must have hated the war.

Strangers were in possession of the aerodromes. Indeed, all the countryside seemed to be reshuffled by the war. Even my garden, where it had always been easy to forget the outside world, did not remain quiet for very long.

On the first day, we might have forgotten the war but for the searchlights at night and the children running home from school with gas masks over their shoulders.

John and I walked along the edge of the clover field, beneath a silver sky and among thousands of white cabbage butterflies darting in the sunlight. The harvest was good and the world seemed calm.

Then the spell broke. Soon after breakfast eight Hurricane fighters rose from the aerodrome, five odd miles away. For me the war had been limited to raids on London and I did not realise the full horror of what was to come. But John knew. He could hear the drone of the German bombers and their escorts coming from the east. We went back to the garden and lay on the grass, with our hands beneath our heads, looking up. John suddenly pointed and said, 'Look!'

A German bomber was hurtling down from the sky, with a scarf of smoke at its tail. It dived into a distant field. We heard the explosion as it hit the ground. Then we looked up. High in the sky, four parachutes were floating down ... lovely, flower-like parachutes, with men swinging to and fro beneath them.

The sound of machine-gun bullets guided our eyes. Over our heads were two formations of bombers surrrounded by fighters ... the fighters darting backwards and forwards so that it was not easy to know if they were ours or theirs. The bombers moved towards the aerodrome and then we heard the thud of the bombs. Debden was getting it.

Then another bomber was flung out of the pattern above us ... flung so that it crashed into a thousand pieces. Then a third fell and the flaming pieces of fuselage made a dangerous rain over the garden. All six of the enemy came down ... before they could recross the coast. Two of ours limped out of the battle and crashed among the distant trees.

We went into the fields to watch the parachutes slowly descending. Then we jumped into the car and sped down the narrow Essex lanes. The hedges bristled with guns. It was strange how the whole countryside had suddenly awakened ... the sleepy acres of farmland became belligerent. We left the car and ran through clover with the old farmers, to wait for the Germans to land. In one hollow we came upon a burning Messerschmitt. I shall never forget the fierce core of the flame. There was no vestige of the crew.

John and I followed an old farmer we knew. He had seen a German land ... the fluttering parachute settling slowly into the stubble. He was a few yards ahead of us, so we left him to his victory.

He peeped through the hedge, to be certain first that his prisoner was not holding a grenade. Centuries of peace had not dulled the edge of his valour or his caution. He was a fine old man, with a beard and quick eyes. He climbed through the hedge and captured his man.

John and I drove back to the house. When we went down to the pub in the evening, John was no longer the only hero in the village. The old farmer was there and he was stealing John's thunder. We gathered about him as he said, 'That German! He was no more than eighteen year old. A boy, you might say. Trembling all over. I was working in the field when they came. And he landed in the next field. I heard tell what they did with they hand grenades so I looked through the hedge first and I saw him walking away, you see, so I ran after him, you see, and I called after him. I said, "Hey!" and he stopped and put his hands up and young George took his revolver and we took him over to the cottage.'

I asked him then, 'Did you feel angry? Did you feel that you would like to shoot him?' He answered, 'No, oh, no. He was a trembling sort of boy. So I just took him back to my cottage until the military came for him. He could not speak English, but he understood when I said, "Cocoa." So my missus made him a cup of cocoa.'

As we drank our beer, the old farmer added a footnote to the story. 'You know, women are queer creatures. All my wife said to me was, "You should have brought home the parachute as well. They're made of fine silk and it would have given me blouses to last me to Doomsday."'

On the way back to the house, John was critical.

'Those cups of cocoa must be stopped,' he said. 'It bolsters up their arrogance.' And then he told me a story. 'Only last week some friends of mine took a German prisoner into the mess and gave him drinks and were kind to him. After he had gone they found out that just before he forced landed, he had flown around one of our pilots while he was descending by parachute and shot him down. These farmers have got to be taught that it isn't all just friendly fun. I have no qualms now in killing Germans. I have seen so many of my own friends shot down that I can't be sentimental any longer.'

37

A new theme came into John's life about this time. He was asked to broadcast and his photograph appeared in newspapers. He was almost a veteran in the Service and the young listened to him with respect.

He had always been shy with other people. Before the war he used to sit in a room, moving his eyes from one speaker to the other with lively interest, but seldom daring to add his own opinion or to raise his voice.

This shyness passed with the first year of the war. I remember a Sunday morning when we went to drink with some friends in London. There was a brilliant barrister, an artist of wit and talent, our host, who was born talking, and several others. John silenced us all as he described the evacuation from Dunkirk. Without any touch of self-consciousness he unfolded the story of the soldiers on the beach, the armada of little boats crossing the Channel, and of the combats in the air.

Eight of us leaned forward, silent and excited. In a slow, serious voice he told his tale. I alone in the room realised the conquest that it stood for, within himself. It was out of this that the new theme in his life slowly grew. His experiences were moulding themselves into wisdom and when he talked he influenced those who were younger than himself.

I do not wish to draw a depressing picture of John as a person without faults. He did not assume this new role without a certain amount of pomp which amused me considerably. He even cleared his throat and behaved like an old oracle in an armchair when youngsters about to join the Service asked for his advice. I smiled within myself, as I watched him assume a stentorian voice to answer their questions. They were not aware of this, nor was he. Nor was it a sign of any decline in his own modesty. It was just a mannerism in a boy who had grown up.

43 Squadron had been moved to Usworth, on the East Coast, while John was on leave. On the last night before he went to join them a young writer came to stay with us. He was John Nesbitt Sellers, a reporter on the staff of *The Times*. John Sellers was a New Zealander and this was our initial bond. He had many talents and a good heart. He wrote quiet, authentic prose and he had already made a name for himself as a speaker over the wireless. He was a tall, awkward creature, with a laugh that came from the pit of his stomach. He bubbled with humour.

John Sellers was on the brink of joining the Air Force. He took all such decisions seriously and he was not casual in his sense of duty. I did not realise, as we sat over our coffee after dinner, that we were repeating the scene of five years before, when John listened to Batchy Atcherley and myself talking of the Service. We, in our turn, called up a lot of pleasant old ghosts and John Sellers listened to us. He wrote to me, when he returned to London, 'Listening to John has made all the difference to my going into the RAF thank you for letting me sit there and hear him talking.'

In October, when John was back with his Squadron, preparing for more victories, John Sellers wrote to me from his Initial Training Wing, 'I am loving it. It is simply grand. Please tell John that some day I hope to see him so that I may salute him, because we are promised our uniforms tomorrow. We are in grand hands. Please tell him that, too, because I would like him to know that I am grateful for all that he said.'

38

The Royal Air Force was faced by a romantic but formidable problem at the end of the first year of the war. The service had to absorb the hundreds of European pilots who came to Britain when their own countries fell before the German invaders. In the early months, Polish and Czech pilots had crossed Europe to join what previously had been an essentially British service. Then came Norwegian, Dutch, Danish and French pilots who escaped to continue their fight in Britain.

The migration of these warriors was overshadowed at the time by reports of battle and disaster. Some day, their story will be gathered together and told in all its majesty.

One morning a French boy of eighteen years came into my office at the Air Ministry. He had gathered petrol together in secret, gallon by gallon, until he had enough to dare to fly to England so that he could fight for France. He had prepared his shaky old aircraft for the flight in the shelter of a wood. And he had flown across, knowing that he would be arrested and more or less certain that he would be fired upon by out anti-aircraft guns. He had never flown beyond the French coast before. Yet he came because he believed that the freedom of his country could be recovered from this island.

One watched the advent of these pilots in amazement. They came, from broken Poland and Czechoslovakia, from unhappy France and from Holland. It was not easy for the Royal Air Force to absorb all of them, with their multitude of tongues. Many squadron and flight commanders in the Air Force found themselves in command of pilots who could not speak a word of English.

This was one of John's problems when he went back to his squadron near Newcastle in September 1940. For the moment, fighting in the air was his second consideration. Czechs and Poles had arrived to be trained into the discipline of 43. Tom Morgan was in command and John, with an old friend, John Kilmartin (Squadron Leader J. T. Kilmartin, DFC. He was with 43 Squadron from 1936 until the beginning of the war when he joined No 1 Squadron to go to France. He returned to 43 Squadron in September 1940), were the flight commanders. They had to reform 43, bringing in new young British pilots and adapting themselves to the temperament of the Czechs and Poles. John's letters during the next few months show how his startled Englishness over the advent of the exiles was slowly broken down and turned to affectionate respect. In his first letter after going back to his squadron, he wrote:

I am as tired as I was two months ago. None of the pilots here are operational. Czechs and Poles for the most part, who cannot speak English and who understand, very little.

Chapter Thirty-Eight

A week or so later, he wrote:

I was wrong about the Czechs and Poles. I suppose I was a bit depressed, finding so many new people. It did not seem like the old 43. I miss Caesar and the others terribly. Thank God for Killie. He is like Laurie in many ways. Nice, unreasonable Irish. He knows all the old jokes and slang and the songs we used to sing. So we are like a couple of old veterans, sighing for the old days and snorting at the young. But I took your lecture to heart. It is very good for all of us having to work and fly with the Czechs and Poles. Their flying is Wizard and they are grand.

Killy has three Poles in A Flight and I have two Czechs in mine. They are Sergeants Sika and Pipa. Nice names, don't you think! Sika and Pipa. They are grand pilots and very keen to go south and have a smack at the Hun.

You were right. The Poles are the most amazing people. They hate so passionately. One of them has a very sad face. Sometimes I see him sitting in the mess, and he runs his hands over his face, and sighs.

And what my two Czechs have been through! I'd like to feel that every Englishman would face the same for his country. These boys went through all that happened in Czechoslovakia, then to fight in France, and then escaped and made their way to this country. It shakes one to the core … seeing patriotism like that. They both wear the Czech war cross and the French Croix de Guerre. Sika, who flies with me as my No 2, is a charmer, but very naughty. Now that we can talk easily I find their sense of humour not so very different from ours. We laugh at the same things. I am teaching him to sing some of the Air Force songs. You should see his face when he tries to sing:

We are the fighting 43
Up from Sussex by the sea ...

His English is now quite good. The Czechs seem to pick it up very quickly. I am going to the Sergeant's mess to drink with them tonight. I'm told that they drink spirits neat.

It has been interesting to see the way everybody now likes them. I suppose we are a lot of stodgy Englishmen, imagining that foreigners are difficult. Now everybody likes the Czechs and the Poles and the ground crew are wonderful with them. All out to help. It is good to see the fitters leap to it and treat Sika and Pipa with just a little more kindness because they are strangers. As Killy says, 'It's a good thing.'

The Poles are very intelligent. Tom Morgan, Killy and I took them to the local last night, and by the end of the evening they had taken possession of the pub. We were given bacon and eggs and beer with the owner and his wife. And they were both so charming to the Poles. They were very touched and the quiet one, who sits in the mess alone, was obviously moved. They kept saying, 'Sank you' and one of them bowed over the pub lady's hand when he said, 'Goodnight.'

Now that we are all settling down, the spirit of the squadron is incredible. After all those knocks! Killy and I feel very pleased about it. The 43 spirit can never die, however much it is mauled.

At the end of November John brought down his tenth enemy aircraft. He wrote the story to me some time afterwards:

Our work here is local defence and the defence of the coastal areas where occasional Huns might snoop about, hoping to tell their

Headquarters the position of our convoys. By catching them in time, before they can transmit the good news, we may ward off a big attack. Sometimes in bad weather, a sneak raider will come in under cover of the cloud and drop a stick of bombs on a shipyard. We are here for all these things, and to rest while we are pulling ourselves together again.

Now I'll tell you what happened. I was at readiness with my flight in the early afternoon. The weather was lousy, low cloud at 200 feet and visibility the width of the aerodrome. It did not seem likely that anything would happen so we were not at instant readiness. We were sitting in the dispersal hut, rather cold, browned off and hating life. I was asked for on the telephone. There was a report of one aircraft off the coast near Newcastle. I was asked if I could send off two aircraft to have a look for it. I did not like the look of the weather so I decided to go alone. The little Czech Sergeant, Sika, was very fussed. He is my No 2, and I find that now we are getting over the language difficulty I understand him much better. He is very keen and his eyes sparkled and then went sad when I said he could not come with me.

I took off through the mist and cloud. It was filthy. I flew out to sea and at about five thousand feet, I emerged into bright sunlight, above the clouds. The surface of the clouds below me was perfectly level. I am told that this has something to do with atmospheric conditions near big industrial areas, but that is all too clever for me. Well, I did not know where I was. I was told over the R/T where to go and after about fifteen minutes I saw an aircraft. It was also flying over the top of the clouds, going east. I felt that it must be a Hun. As I closed on him I recognised it as a Ju 88. I was about a quarter of a mile away and above him. Apparently he had not seen me. I closed in, fired and hit his starboard motor. He dived for the clouds, but I fired again from closer quarters. This stopped his starboard engine and pieces fell from his port wing root. He waffled in the air banked over and dived steeply into the clouds. It was too risky in that weather to follow him. So I fixed my position over the R/T and returned with some difficulty. I could only claim a 'probable' but I hoped that that dive was his last. Fortunately for me, the Hun had crashed through the cloud into the sea, near to a trawler. The captain reported that a Ju 88 had crashed near by and as the time was the same my 'probable' became a 'destroyed.'

39

About this time there was a complaint in some of the newspapers that the ground crews of the Royal Air Force were not being sufficiently honoured. I do not think the question ever arose among the older squadrons of the Service. I went to stay with 43 for a few days late in the winter of 1940 and I realised, as well as anybody bent over a desk in the Air Ministry can realise, the pride and faith that held the flying personnel and the ground crews together.

One afternoon, I went down to the drab, weatherboarded dispersal huts and talked to the fitters and riggers who had been with 43 since the beginning of the war.

The war teaches one great lesson to those of us who are amateurs in blue. We learn that the word *service* is not merely preacher's talk. We do learn to serve something beyond our own ideals, which are so often merely forged out of mental arrogance.

The fitters and riggers of 43 Squadron understood what *service* means. One of them, a tough, silent little man from Northumberland said, 'I never feel that I do enough.'

I talked also to a flight-rigger who was equally warm with pride. He told me of a night when he was called out, after a long day of work, to change a flap of an aircraft which was to fly early next morning. He worked all night. When I asked him, 'Wasn't that a little too much after working all day?' he said, 'Oh, no! You see, there is no squadron like ours. And the pilots depend on us more than anything. They have a sort of faith in us. And after all, it is our job to keep as many aircraft in the front line as possible, and, of course, you get to know the machine you are working on. You never do the same job twice and you never want to change your pilot or your machine. You see, you learn the pilot's eccentricities. You see, some like flying with the left wing low, some with the right wing low and some horizontal. You just get to know them, you see and, well, it is all part of the squadron, see!'

Then I spoke to John's rigger who had looked after his Hurricane all through the battles of the months before. He was the age of 43, but behind his deluge of slang and his quick little eyes was a zeal which seemed to prick one's own mind to fresh wakefulness. He had patched the hole in John's aircraft after he shot down his first Hun off the East Coast. He said that he had been a bit 'browned off' after leaving Tangmere. There was a lull while the squadron was reforming and he did not enjoy rest. He was terribly proud because 43 had shot down so many. 'It gives you an old school tie sort of feeling,' he said.

Then he talked of the old days at Tangmere and in the North of Scotland. 'We had bags of excitement there,' he said. 'I remember when they brought down a Heinkel when the Germans were raiding Scapa Flow.' Then he added his version of the story I have already told, when the Heinkel landed on the flare path imagining that it was landing in the sea. The rigger said, 'It crashed on the flare path ... the stupid twirps thought they was over the sea. But our boys got them that night. We had to turn the flare path round to let all the other kites come in.'

Then he told me of a day when a Dornier came over. 'You know, when Operations tell us to take cover we take our rifles with us and go to the dugout. Well, this day, the Dornier came well within rifle range and my mate and I got in ten rounds apiece. I hope we hit him. The Hurricanes brought it down, but I felt that I was a bit of an ace after that.'

I tried to make him talk of his own work, but it existed only as part of the work of the pilots. 'The most interesting time is when they come back from action. We all clamour round. There are bags of excitement when our pilots have brought some Jerries down. And then you look for bulletholes, because you become sort of attached to your own kite. I suppose it's like a groom with a horse.'

Then, without a trace of self-consciousness, he said 'You see, our squadron is rather exceptional, isn't it?'

I think the riggers and fitters helped me to understand, as combat reports and stories of valour never have done the mystery that gives a squadron its tradition and its heart. At that time, young pilots were arriving in 43 from training units, half fledged and eager, only to be posted away when 43 had taught them how to take their place in the battle. Pilots came and went almost every week. But the squadron kept its integrity and individuality.

I sometimes think that those devoted men of the ground, who followed the squadron from station to station, seeing pilots fight and die, or pass on to other squadrons, are the real guardians of that tradition.

John once told me that when he censored the airmen's letters he often came on the phrase, 'We brought down another today.' Perhaps the word *we* is the key to all I'm trying to say.

40

The word *party* has a special meaning for older members of the Royal Air Force. It does not necessarily call for invitations, lights and many people. Seven or eight pilots sitting in a room, tippling and talking and singing, may have a party, if the spirit that is with them is right. The number of pilots in 43 who could have a party in the old sense of the word had become very few. When I went to stay with the squadron, now and then, I felt that an age of time had fallen upon them in little more than a year.

One evening I spent with 43 is clear in my memory. There were only Tom Morgan, Kilmartin and John left of the older ones. And there was Knockers North, who also came into the picture because he had been with the squadron almost a year.

Tom Morgan, Killy, Knockers, John and I stood before the fire, laughing and sighing over what had been. It seemed to me that the whole pattern of the changed Air Force was spread in that room, with its dilapidated armchairs, its ubiquitous RAF carpet and the mantelpiece upon which we rested our glasses.

Tom Morgan was English to the core: modest, fiercely proud of the Service, devoted to his wife and certain of his own ideas. His was the Englishness that cannot boast. He commanded 43 and kept its spirit high, through terrible vicissitudes.

Next to the typical Englishman was John, not so typically English ... but more English than anything else. A man who had killed the enemy without losing the gentleness of his own spirit.

And then dear Knockers North, a New Zealander after my own heart, with whom I could gossip about the beauties of the

Southern Alps and the joy of New Zealand fish and butter. 'A frightfully brave little chap' is the way John always described him. He had been ill, with his kidneys, and he had been badly shot up in the Battle of Britain. His back and arms were riddled with pieces of shrapnel. He would pinch little points of steel out of his arm, like blackheads. His body was a perpetual distress to him. He had two rows of false teeth and a face that laughed all the time. He was only twenty-four, but his hair was grey and if his face had ever rested from smiling I think he would have looked very old.

And Kilmartin! I don't think one can say anything about Killy except that he is Irish. That implies charm, casualness, courage and a loyalty to his friends which is a form of religion. There was a fifth figure, on the edge of the scene. The Polish pilot of whom John had written was sitting at the back of the room, alone and silent. I don't think he was conscious of our chatter. He still ran his hands over his face, nursing the bitter memory of Warsaw and the perpetual sorrow of separation from his wife and children. The only way he could answer these feelings within himself was with moroseness when he was on the earth, and terrible hatred when he was in the sky.

There we were, in that rather dreary room; two Englishmen, two New Zealanders, an Irishman, and a Pole, wearing the same blue uniform, stirred with the same faith and believing in the same laws of kindness.

We had been laughing over the old days. John recalled a mad afternoon in the North of Scotland when they all went to the local cinema. The attraction was the next episode of *Riders of the Wild West*. Caesar, Eddie Edmonds and Tony Woods-Scawen had been following the adventures of the hero from week to week. They would land after a combat near Scapa Flow and rush into the town to see the new episode. One afternoon, they went armed with cap pistols which they had bought in a toyshop. Every time there was gunfire in the film the pilots in the dress circle let off their toy pistols. The manager tapped Caesar on the shoulder and said that they must either pocket their pistols or leave.

The story set us remembering. Killie said, 'Let's have a real 43 party.' So they took me off to the neighbouring town and we drank and laughed and talked. And it was a party. But the Pole would not come. 'No sank you,' he said, 'I will stay and learn some more of my English.'

41

The time came for John to hand on his experience to the young. During these months, when the Service was growing so swiftly in numbers, generations in the Air Force were separated by years and not by decades. We all doted on the word expansion. Pilots in their twenties were already senior and responsible. John was then twenty-seven and he was the veteran of his squadron.

So the day came for him to be posted away, to command a squadron of his own and to assume the field rank of Squadron Leader. Ranks in the Air Force are still a muddle to the man in the street. It meant that John was a major and that the time had come for him to be a father to the Volunteer Reserve pilots who were pouring in and forming the majority of the Service.

Early in December 1940, John wrote:

Ha! ha! You will now have to call me sir and salute me. But I think you will be pleased. I am to be a Squadron Leader. It is all very exciting. I have been posted to command a squadron of my own. They are in Northern Ireland. All I know is that they formed at the beginning of the war and that they have had very little action and excitement. It is a hell of a responsibility, but I am determined to do it bloody well. I shall model them on all that I have learned in 43. But I feel terrible about leaving 43. It's five years now. And those five years have taught me all I know about fighting, comradeship and love of my fellow men. I have been Adjutant, Flight Commander and Second-in-Command. When the war came I fought in most of the battles with them. But now as I leave, there are few of the old ones I know.

I am the oldest member and ever since the war began I have dearly wanted to command 43. When Caesar was killed I would have loved to follow him as CO but it was right that Tom Morgan should do it as he was senior. And he is a magnificent person. I think 43's spirit is quite safe in his hands. But I go away hoping that I might still come back and follow in the place of George, Tubby Badger and Caesar.

When the news came everyone was charming. Tom told me and congratulated me and said that he was sorry that it was not 43 that I was going to command. Think of that … and he is commanding it himself!

I have learned much from him, although he is four years younger than I am, and has been in the squadron for only a matter of months. He has never done anything without talking it over with me. He always says 'We.' 'What shall *we* do?' 'Don't you think *we* …' always. He is one of the best squadron commanders I could possibly imagine. He stands no nonsense from anyone. He has taught me to be determined with my ideas. I think that is important. Having an idea and believing in it and walking over everything and everyone to see that it is carried out. I am not in the least afraid of my new job.

If I can teach them to be like 43, I shall be all right!

So John and his luggage were flown across the Irish Channel in an Anson and his new work began. I remember him saying that he felt 'rather shy.' In a note which I seem to have lost he told me that he kept looking at the three stripes on his sleeve, hardly believing that they were true. And his embarrassment when the Flight Lieutenant who flew him called him 'sir.'

In his first letter from Ireland John wrote:

I am now beginning to settle down. The first few days were very hectic and I got to know no one in the squadron. The old CO had been promoted to Wing Commander and he stayed for three days to hand the squadron over to me. My introduction to the squadron meant a succession of parties from the pilots, the sergeants and the troops. I had no time to get to know anyone. But it is all a bit terrifying because even while I was taking over, signals arrived every day, posting some of my pilots overseas. It means that I am losing the backbone of the squadron and I shall have to begin at the beginning. I can quite understand them wanting to be posted. There has been nothing doing here for ages and they all feel a bit browned off. So they naturally jump at the chance of being posted to Egypt or any place where there is likely to be some action. I have managed to get Chipper Chaffe (Flying Officer R. I. Chaffe was afterwards posted to command a squadron in Malta and was lost on his way out) from 43. Imagine what this means because I can build up something with him. He will make a good flight commander in time. He is full of self discipline. Never smokes or drinks and is awfully fit. My senior Flight Commander leaves today and a tough New Zealander who I hardly know is taking over his flight. His name is Mowat (now Squadron Leader Mowat, DSO). There is one person who I like instinctively. I feel he will be a tremendous help because he has accepted me straight away. His name is Kitson. He is a shy boy from Lancashire, terribly keen, and an excellent flyer. I found out the reason today for his mad determination. His brother was in the Air Force, in Bomber Command. He was in a raid over the Baltic and lost both his eyes. He was piloting a Hampden. The brother is at St Dunstans, learning Braille and things like that. He is completely blind.

Kitson is terribly devoted to his brother and he told me that when he goes to see him at St Dunstans, he is so embarrassed and terribly unhappy because the brother stumbles and falls over and loses his temper.

There are four Czechs in the squadron. One of them is an officer named Perniker. He is almost forty and so brave and determined. I feel quite an old hand at dealing with the Czechs now. I think I understand them!

In another note, John wrote:

I really feel rather grand. I have a pleasant room of my own and a bathroom and I can ask the boys in to talk quietly and have a drink. I get to know them that way and they talk more easily. Kitson comes and talks. He makes me feel like the old days with 43. He is so loyal and intelligent. I feel more confident about the future of the Service with pilot officers of his type coming on.

I found out what a good type he is by one thing. You know that the squadron has been out of the battle since Dunkirk. They feel that they are in a backwater here. And they are keen. Kitson, who has been with the squadron for a long time, asked me if I would speak to the troops. He said that as I had just come from England it would mean something to them. They sit here and hear of their families being blitzed in England and I suppose they feel out of it. It was nice of Kitson to think of it. The whole squadron was paraded in a hangar, in their overalls. About two hundred or so.

It just shows what a democratic service we are. The Warrant Officer introduced me to the squadron. There were no other officers there. Just myself, the Warrant Officer and the troops called to attention. I told the Warrant Officer to tell them to stand at ease. His introduction was very nice. Something about your new CO who, if I may say so, sir, has had great experience.

I think I said what was right. I told them I knew that they wanted to go south and be in the battle, I said I was anxious to go with them, but that before I took them south I wanted to have new aircraft and I wanted the squadron to be fully operational.

Of course, the trouble is that there are so many new pilots who have got to be taught to fight. I told them that. And I told them that they had to be patient. I was pretty strong-minded with them then and I told them that as long as they did not try to hoodwink me I would play fair with them. They are a decent lot of chaps and I think it won't be long before we do something. I said at the end that I would not be a hard CO, but that equally, I was not weak-minded and that they must not try to pull a fast one on me. I think I pulled them together as a squadron. They broke up and went on with their work as I walked out. I walked out alone and back to my office.

The Adjutant, a delightful person named John Denman, was there. Kitson was there too. And Chaffe. They were censoring letters. They asked me how the talk went and just then the Warrant Officer walked in and said, 'That went off all right, sir, if you don't mind my saying so.'

I honestly think it was a good beginning. Please forgive me for shooting a bit of a line but I must let off steam to someone.

After a week or so had passed, John wrote:

I spend all my time with my squadron. They are my only interest over here. I am very proud of them now. They are all good boys, keen and bright, and ready to fight. I am like an old hen fussing them about.

42

In January and February of 1941, John's squadron was training for full-scale operations and during the first few weeks I heard little from him. There is only his logbook to record the details of his flying and the intensive training of his pilots. But I heard from friends that the formation flying of the squadron was perfect. In peace time 43 had always been celebrated for its formation flying and John was handing the talent on. He wrote to me once in late January:

I have been sitting in the office for two hours working like a black, and I thought I might send you some news. I sit here, at a big desk, with the adjutant opposite me. I have told you about him before.

He is John Denman, a wizard. There is a window through which I can see the aircraft ready to take off and the pilots sitting outside their dispersal hut in the sun. I am able to keep my eye on them, when they take off and when they land. I can even see them firing their guns over Loch Neagh. Kit and Chipper are marvellous. When they are not at readiness, they spend all their time training the boys in the air.

Sometimes at night they both come into my room and talk. A night or two ago, they were there and Chipper said something which was pleasing. He said it was amazing how much I had made the squadron like 43. You remember that he was with me in 43. He said I had done it without any apparent effort. Kitson said that the squadron had changed since I had been there. 'You seem to love the Air Force, don't you?' he said. 'I hope you realise how much you have made us love it too. Not only making us part of it. You explain everything in such a different way. What you said playing snooker tonight. I bet it will make a hell of a difference to Denys and Peter.'

That pleased me.

I am a bit pompous and fussy I am afraid. I must be growing old. I find myself watching everything they do and if any dimmy is about to land with his wheels up, I rush out, very alarmed, to see whether the flight commanders have popped off any Verey lights or done anything about it. Thank God they always do, so we are still without an accident, touch wood.

Chipper and Kit were in the office yesterday and we decided that we should have a plant or some flowers to cheer it up. When I went in this morning the plant was there – something like a geranium but not quite. Chipper and Kit had brought it back last night. But it had a very short life. Chipper has a minute puppy. An Irish water-hound. Just a curly black ball. It is a sweet, affectionate little thing and it bites your fingers. It was sitting on the windowsill in the sun. It stood up, very solemnly, saw the flower, walked over and ate it, just like Ferdinand the bull. We photographed it.

George Lott flew over to see me the other day. It was fun to see him again. He was sitting in my office, having a good natter about the old days when a dimmy taxied in with his flaps still down. I saw it through the window so I jumped to it. I sent for him and I tore him off a hell of a strip. George said that I was shooting a line and being grand. But he did admit that this is probably the reason why we have no accidents. I really think the squadron is thoroughly pulled together now and ready to fight anywhere, with anyone.

On 3 February, John took a few days leave and flew to Blackpool, with the senior controller at Aldergrove, to bring Kitson back from leave. His letter emphasises the ability of pilots to fling themselves quickly from the stern ritual of duty into the nonsense of a holiday. He wrote to me, on 6 February:

We have been working all out and I thought a spot of leave would not do us any harm. So I asked the Station Commander for 48 hours to have a jolly. I took MacEwen with me, to bring Kit back. We left about 11 in the morning in the Blenheim. We have one … I don't know if I have ever told you. When the squadron was formed they were equipped with Blenheims converted as twin-engine fighters. When they came to Ireland, with their Hurricanes, they had one Blenheim left, and the squadron kept it for collecting spares from England and to take myself and my flight commanders to conferences.

Kit had found rooms for Mac and myself at St Annes. It was funny seeing Blackpool from the air, looking just the same as in peace time. The Blackpool Tower was sticking out of a haze. It is a comic place.

Kit met us with his father's car at the aerodrome. He was born in Lancashire so he acted as guide and drove us about to see the sights. I wish you had been there. It was such a complete break. I haven't enjoyed myself so much for years. We started off at Wonderland, the immense building with cinemas, theatres, restaurants, a ballroom and fourteen bars. Have you ever seen it? I am afraid that we went to all the bars in turn. It was our first party for ages. Some of the bars were very funny, oldy worldy, rather bogus and filled with most extraordinary people, a bit hot and smelly. When we went upstairs to eat we were feeling very gay, laughing, just because we were happy. Kit flopped into his chair and when he looked at the menu he just said, 'Can't read a word. Make it *fisssssh*!'

I can't put the hiss of the way he said it on paper.

Well, It was *fisssssh*, which was odd. It did not taste like any *fisssssh* I have ever had before.

Then we went to the ballroom and watched the people whirling around. After a time we decided it wasn't good for our heads – the whirling. But it was beautiful. A great mass of people, waltzing and a very good band. Much more beautiful than those old body clutchers at the Dorchester, dancing cheek to cheek. But our heads were a bit sensitive to the whirling and the heat so we had to call it a day. We had to take the air. We walked along the sea front and Kit suddenly talked broad Lancashire to us. Very champion. We could see hundreds of couples flirting on the sand. The sea air was a bit strong and we felt rather fragile. So Kit drove us back to our rooms at St Annes. Then he went back to his father. He didn't say anything about his brother. I think he takes it very badly.

Next morning it was lovely and we felt as fit as hell. We simply had to fly, so we telephoned Kit and he hurried over. We jumped into the Blenheim and flew to see 43. It was so perfect, although most of the country seemed to be cotton mills and mines. But the sky was perfect, with those lovely white cumulus clouds like teased cotton wool. I played with the clouds, diving through. them and rushing into little gaps before they could close up.

Tom Morgan and Killy were a bit rude about my arriving in the Blenheim. Killy said something about my shooting a line by arriving in a 'bloody great thing like that.'

Then they did a charming thing. They had had a silver mug made for me with the 43 crest. Just as we were taking off Tom handed it to me full of beer. We all made a loving cup of it.

We took off from Drem expecting to arrive back at Aldergrove before dark. But the weather became filthy and we flew through storms and got ourselves thoroughly lost. I became rather frightened. We found Carlisle and landed at an aerodrome nearby when it was almost dark.

We found rooms in the town at the Crown and Mitre. While we were having a drink Kit disappeared. It was so like him. He had been out to a shop and bought us each a toothbrush and one tube of toothpaste, just because he realised that they would be closing soon.

We got back to Aldergrove next morning and now we are working our guts out again.

43

In March 1941, John wrote:

The two Polish officers with me were shy in the beginning. They stayed together and were merely polite when I spoke to them. I think that I have overcome this. Indeed, I know I have. I took them both to a pub in Belfast and they were much better then. They talked quite freely and I made a joke or two. A little understanding seems to help. Kit has been a great help to me in this. He is so very understanding with them and with the Czechs. If we are drinking at night he always asks if he can fetch them to join us. He says they must be a bit lonely.

One has simply to realise that they feel and think differently from us and therefore deal with them differently. It is no use our expecting to make Englishmen of them. They are really very grateful for anything you do for them. They showed it in what they did about my car.

I was the only person here with a car, the staff one. It is always difficult to get about in this part of the world, so I bought a squadron car, a very old Austin 7 Saloon, for five pounds. You know the sort of rattletrap. There are always three or four outside the best messes. Koc, one of my Polish boys, asked me if he could mend it and smarten it up. I said he could and he and most of the boys set about it in the hangar. I said nothing and left them to it. But I was a bit shaken when I saw Koc sawing the hood off that evening. It looked as if the car had had it. But I passed on. Then I went away to Dublin for a few days (Oranges and steaks).

When I got back Koc came to the office and asked me if I would inspect the car. It was covered over with a tarpaulin so we had a proper unveiling ceremony. Chipper, Kit, Brian, Peter, Dennis and John drew the tarpaulin off, very solemnly, and there was a two-seater sports model Austin. Koc had done most of the work. He had built the body out of metal from the scrap dump and he had fitted a windscreen from a derelict Hayford aeroplane. The boys had painted it green and brown. They had taken the engine to pieces and repaired it with broken aeroplane parts. I stepped into it with Koc for a trial run on the tarmac. It went like a bird and we touched 50 mph we have painted the squadron crest on it and I have handed it over as the squadron car. They take it in turns, for parties in Belfast.

The Poles are very earnest and grateful.

In the middle of March 1941, the Poles were posted away to join one of their own squadrons. John told me the story over the telephone. It was inspiring to build up the picture of these lonely pilots, with no news from their country and every bond with their old life depending upon their heart and their memory, flying across the Irish Channel, escorted by three of the squadron Hurricanes. John wrote in a letter:

We left like a royal party. I still have the Blenheim. Kit suggested that we should fly the Poles to their new station in the north of England. I flew, with Kit beside me and the Poles and their luggage in the bomb well. One of the controllers, who also wanted to come for a ride, sat in the gun turret. We were really gay. I felt pleased because all the barriers had been broken down, but terribly sad at losing them. They did not know what my feelings were. I have a continuous sense of frustration, meeting new pilots, knowing them and flying with them. Then liking them and losing them.

We were six in the Blenheim, with luggage. We shouted at each other but couldn't hear much. The Hurricanes flew round us in formation until we had crossed the Irish Sea. Sometimes they were so close that I could see Chipper's eager face. He gave us the two finger sign. It was a murky day, with clouds at about 3,000 feet. There was enough, sun to show up the beauty of the hills between West Freugh and Carlisle.

It was rather nice when we landed them at X. The Poles were obviously delighted. They kept saying 'Sank you, sank you.'

The Pole you met at Usworth was on the tarmac. They are forming another Polish squadron there. When, they are together you notice the keenness and the devotion to each other that they've got. It's being exiles I suppose.

It's their gratitude I like. Their manners ... a sort of mad gratitude because we are giving them an opportunity to fight the Hun. I think the war would be over much sooner if the English could be taught to hate as much as they do.

We flew on late in the afternoon to have a drink with 43. Tom and Killy and Stuart Cary were there. We hurried to the mess. I rather felt that I was shooting a line, bringing my good types with me to show them. I must say I felt a bit proud, being able to point out that my squadron had done more flying hours than any other in the Group and that we had not had one accident. Killy told me to pipe down. He and Tom Morgan attacked me viciously for shooting a line.

It was dark when we arrived back at Aldergrove. I had to hand over to Kit as I have never landed a two-engine machine in the dark. He had, so it was all right. I was much too frightened to try it myself.

44

Up to this time, the war had not touched Northern Ireland except with rumour and suspicion. The Germans had allowed it to simmer in doubt: But, in the spring of 1941, they made a bombing attack on Belfast and the city blazed under enemy action for the first time. John's squadron were still at Aldergrove and, in the action of 8 April, he brought down the first German aircraft over Northern Ireland.

John wrote me a long letter a few days afterwards:

I was in the mess when news came through that the Germans were approaching Belfast. It came as a surprise, because you know how peaceful it has been here. Incendiaries had been dropped and high explosives were on the way. It was about 1.15 in the morning. I ran out to find that it was very dark, with a sickly moon shining through a mist. As I ran to the dispersal point I could see and hear the guns of Belfast ... the flashes in the sky. It had already begun. Two other aircraft took off and I was third in the squadron. I climbed to about 9,000 feet, passing above the clouds. The moon was in its second quarter and it shone out of a blue-black sky, peppered with stars. Below me was the floor of clouds like silver-grey snow.

I flew towards the south, away from Belfast, to meet the Huns coming up the coast. I was told that there were enemy aircraft there. It seemed ages as I flew on and on. My eyes searched the blackness. There was no horizon and no object upon which to fix my eyes. I had the illusion, as I travelled at two hundred miles an hour, that all the stars were moving ... as if they were the taillights of aircraft. I searched among the moving pattern of lights and my eyes rested on two black objects. I could see them because, as they moved, they obliterated the stars.

It was an amazing scene ... the Kingdom of the Heavens ... with the two objects moving a little above me. They were quite near when I recognised them as aircraft. Whether enemy or not, I was unable to tell. So I flew nearer and learned soon enough. The rear gunners of both aircraft fired on me apparently at the same time. There was a shower of bullets, some with the whitish-green light of tracer bullets, some glowing red. Perhaps incendiaries. Thank God they missed me. It was very frightening. It was my first experience of being fired on in the dark and I didn't like it.

For a minute I lost the Huns as I took avoiding action. But I had to find them again. Then I saw them again, flying farther apart and moving against the white floor of the clouds below me. They were black and quite clear, silhouettes, just definite enough for me to know that they were Heinkels.

The advantage was now mine for they were perfectly placed as targets. I crept down to attack the rearmost of them. They were flying very slowly then and it was difficult for me to withhold my speed so that I would not overtake them; I came in gently and I opened fire from slightly below.

Then came my next surprise. I have never fired my guns in the dark before. There was a god awful flash, quite blinding. In daylight one does not see it. At night it is terrific and I was so blinded that I lost sight of my Hun.

He had gone into a gentle dive towards the clouds and for a moment I thought he was lost. He increased his speed and, this made it easier for me to attack. I was able to close in. He was in a perfect position for me so I opened fire once more. It was closer range than before. This time I was prepared for the flash of my guns and I kept my eyes on him. His rear gunner returned my fire, but only for a second I had apparently got him for he was silent after that. Nothing more came so I was able to close in still more and continue my fire.

Then I saw a comforting red glow in his belly. Below the glow was hanging an immense object. I could see the silhouette of it. I suppose it must have been a very heavy bomb or a mine and I think I must have hit it. I was still firing when the Heinkel blew up, with a terrific explosion which blew me upwards and sideways. I found out afterwards that bits of metal from the Hun had hit my left wing and had made a tear in the fuselage by the tail plane.

When I righted myself, I was delighted to see showers of flaming pieces, like confetti on fire. We were now over the sea and I could see the little flaming bits falling through the cloud below me.

I had travelled twenty or thirty miles during the combat. I was a bit shaken, but when my mind was quiet again I was able to enjoy the satisfaction of knowing that I had brought the bastard down before he had dropped his bombs on Belfast. Curious feeling of pleasure in this.

The second Heinkel had disappeared. In any case I could not have done much about it as my ammunition was rather low. So I asked for homing instructions over the R/T.

I spoke to George Knox who was controlling and told him of my success. I could hear over the R/T he and the whole Ops room seemed to go mad. You see, it meant a lot to them for it was their first victory (the squadron were lodgers on a Coastal Command Station. A fighter victory was unique on a station whose combats were all with submarines far out m the Atlantic). George said he had seen the Hun's track suddenly disappear off the map in the Control Room. He said 'It's too good to be true.' He asked me all about it over the R/T, which was rather naughty. And he said there would be a party for me when I landed.

As I turned for home, I could see the anti-aircraft shells bursting above Belfast and the glow of the fires on the clouds. It was a bit horrible. When one knows a town and when you drink in its pubs, it hurts a bit to think of it being bombed. The incendiaries had done their bloody worst and I could see that Belfast had been pasted badly.

I flew back and landed quickly as the flare path could not be left on for too long or the Huns would have found our aerodrome and we would have got it.

Of course my ground crew knew all about my victory before I landed. Ops had rung up dispersal. The crew ran out to my wing tips to guide me in. They put their thumbs up at me to let me know. The fitters and riggers were so nice to me when I jumped out and my senior armament NCO was almost in tears with pleasure. His name is Humphries. Such a nice chap and so keen.

Kit, and Pilley, my Intelligence Officer, were yelling with delight and they cried out *Wizard* in the dark. I must say I was thrilled.

Chipper was still flying and we hoped he might have got one too, but I am afraid he didn't.

If you are writing anything, please try to say something about the ground crews and what they do. People are a little too apt to give all the credit to the pilots and the newspapers should be told. I felt the importance of this very much when I went over to the hangar the morning after, or the same morning to be precise.

On the side of my aircraft are the swastikas, one for each of my victories. Before my crew went off they had painted the eleventh swastika on the side of the cockpit.

Well, there it is. The first one over Northern Ireland. I can't help feeling a bit pleased.

45

The time was coming for John's squadron to prove itself in the battles of the South. He wrote to me in March of 1941, 'I am applying for leave on 10 April. Couldn't we meet somewhere in Wales? My squadron is magnificent, but I am tired and want a rest before we begin fighting.'

Two weeks later he wrote again:

I shall be arriving at Port Merrion on the afternoon of 12 April. I am coming by air and bringing Kit who is going to stay with his father and brother for the weekend. It is nearly spring and I have just seen my first daffodil. I am so poor.

I must tell you about Kit. We were playing snooker last night. He makes me play a game every night because he says it is good for me. When I do well he puts on a strong Lancashire accent and says 'That was champion.' He told me that all these months, he has been saving a little each week to buy an electric guitar for his brother. I think I told you before that he was blinded after a raid on Kiel. Now he has no pleasure except music and Kit has gone without many things to do this for him. So I shall be bringing him over, plus his electric guitar.

I travelled to Port Merrion in a slow meandering train and I met John on the shores of Port Merrion estuary in the afternoon.

He had brought Kitson, MacEwen (son of Air Vice-Marshal N. D. K. MacEwen, CB, CMG, DSO), his senior controller, and his engineer officer. Kit stepped out of the Blenheim, clutching his guitar and took MacEwen off to his home.

The plan was to leave John in Wales for a week. The others were to return to Ireland in the Blenheim, after their weekend.

I had not seen John for five months and during this time, he had reformed his squadron. He was definite and self-assured. We walked along the shore of the estuary. It was a placid April day and the slopes beside that lovely water were gay with rhododendrons and daffodils. We tried to recapture the art of being lazy.

I think that John's work during the previous months had brought him more happiness and fulfilment than his combats. He talked of the young pilots like an old father. They had come to trust him with their troubles and he knew and studied them separately, with new comprehension of the vagaries of human nature. 'But I have been very firm,' he said. 'I have never hesitated to get rid of a pilot who held up the squadron or who was troublesome.'

When we went into the bar of the hotel, John's uniform and DFC attracted the attention of the old ladies who were sheltering from the war. I smiled a little at the benevolent note in his voice when he answered their questions. He almost verged on the pompous, which amused me. There was a charming and intelligent man from Liverpool staying in the hotel. He talked to John for a long time. Next morning he said to me, 'your friend helps me to understand the character of the Air Force. I know now why they do so well.'

That night we drank champagne. We were rather poor so the extravagance was pleasant.

As I lay in bed, with the window open and the faint moonlight etching the outlines of the estuary, I could not help flinging my thoughts back again to the ship coming home from Australia. As I lay there, enjoying my pride over the conquests of a friend, I heard droning in the night. A big wave of German aircraft passed over the water.

John told me next morning that he supposed they were on their way to bomb Northern Ireland.

We passed two lazy days, tramping over the hills and gliding about the estuary in a little boat. A kind and charming couple from Cheshire, Mr and Mrs Porrit, had a cottage by the water and we sat with them and talked. We spun reckless notions of what we would do when the war was over. I remember that John asked for no more than to return to his farm in Huntingdonshire. He was never more nor less than an Englishman fighting for England. For him, the issue was simple. I remember him saying, with a fierce note in his voice, 'All I care about is winning the war.' He meant it, with an Englishman's passion for the security and freedom of his own earth.

It was already rare to know pilots who had survived almost two years of the war. Their faces had changed and their eyes seemed to search restlessly beyond the immediate scene. There was some aura about them, independent of hero worship. They walked apart from the men of the earth. I felt this about John as he moved among the kind old ladies and the ancient colonels, cuddling their memories.

They were two perfect days. But it was not time to judge the play for the play was not yet done. During the morning of the third day, John was called to the telephone. He came back into the garden and told me, in a cold, voice, that the Blenheim had taken off from Blackpool with Kit and Mac. But it had crashed and they were killed.

I did not speak to him. I let him walk away. He told me afterwards, 'I walked far into the fields and sat down in the sunlight and sobbed.' And then, 'I would not have minded so much if they had been killed in action. I know all about that. But it seems such terrible waste, losing them in a bloody silly little accident like that.'

So our leave ended. John went back to Ireland and I got on to the train again and came back to London. I remember that the bombs were already falling as we came to Paddington. It was the night of a terrible raid and the Thames ran red from the fires on its banks.

46

In the weeks that followed new pilots arrived to strengthen the squadron and John's letters became short, busy notes. He told me some time afterwards of the day when he flew across to the English coast to attend Kit's funeral. He said, 'His father and mother were there. They asked me to climb on to the lorry where the coffin was lying and place some flowers over Kit's heart. I climbed up and did it but I did not like it.'

When John returned to Ireland from the funeral, Chipper was waiting for him. John wrote of this:

We are just going ahead as before. Chipper was there as we landed and he said, 'I hope everything went off all right, sir. Everything is OK here.' The boys were in good form and no one was depressed.

On 6 May John brought down his second enemy aircraft over Northern Ireland. It was the night of a big and sustained effort by the enemy and the sky was alive with aircraft. He wrote of this:

I was about fourth or fifth in the squadron to go up. Somewhere around 2.30 in the morning. There was thick cloud at three thousand feet and above it a full moon. It is unpleasant flying through cloud. And it is worse still at night. But when you emerge through the top, the beauty and serenity of the moonlight on the tops of the grey clouds takes your breath away.

My only means of knowing my position was by my R/T messages to and from George, who was controlling. He was always good at night and he made me feel that he really understood our feelings as we flew in the dark. He had a comforting sort of voice, telling me that *he* knew all right where I was.

I found three enemy aircraft flying loosely together. I shot one of them down. But it was not an exciting combat because I was frightened and worried about getting home. I have always had this fear when flying above clouds at night. I was more frightened still this time, because in the excitement I let off a parachute flare hoping to take a cine-camera film of my flaming Hun. I did not realise that this would show up my position to other enemy aircraft. It was a foolish thing to do. Of course someone got on my tail right away and followed me home. He fired on me, but thank God he missed.

Chapter Forty-Six

I had been given a course to steer for base and I had been told to remain above the clouds. Soon after the enemy finished attacking, I was told that I was over base and that I could break cloud.

I dived into the clouds, back towards the ugly world, hoping that I had been well looked after ... that I would be over the aerodrome. But there was a mistake of ten miles in my position and the one thing I dreaded had happened.

I came out of the cloud at 2,000 feet and circled over some lights below me. They were not the aerodrome lights or the flares. They were the fires from the bombs that had been dropped on Belfast and I was flying among the barrage balloons. I could do nothing but fly straight on and hope for the best. I have always dreaded hitting a balloon cable. It would be a poor sort of way to end.

Well, I was lucky. I escaped and landed at base feeling very sick. I am tired, I suppose I could not write my combat report so Pilley did it for me. Then I went to bed. I forgot to get up in the morning. I slept for twenty hours without a break.

When I woke up in the afternoon, I was conscious of a strong smell of fish. On a table in the corner of the room were three dozen oysters and a pint of Guinness. The others had put them there while. I was asleep, with a little note, 'With love from your boys.'

I went into Belfast in the evening to have my hair cut. The barber was silent until the end. Then he said, 'It is a pity none of you shot down any of the enemy last night.' I paid, grabbed my hat and left.

47

Early in May, after the four-day blitz of Northern Ireland, John wrote:

The people in Belfast were badly shaken by the bombing and have been very Irish about it. Yesterday the Duke and Duchess of Gloucester arrived to see the damage and to talk to the people who have lost their homes. They flew and landed on our aerodrome. The boys were all lined up and as the Duke and Duchess stepped out of the aircraft, the station band played God Save the King. I felt very sentimental – seeing them come so simply and hearing the anthem. The squadron commanders were introduced to them and I was made quite a showpiece because of my two Huns. The Duchess was very charming about it. She was very intelligent about the Service and said that she would like to see my aircraft.

It was on the tarmac, nearby. She looked at my swastikas and then she wanted to climb in. I dissuaded her because she was wearing her best blue as an Air Commandant in the WAAF.

My crew told me afterwards that they were slightly hurt over this, as the aircraft was spotless.

We had a small luncheon party for them in the mess and I sat next to the Duchess. I introduced her to Chipper and Brian before lunch and they said afterwards: 'My God, what a wonderful person.' She was almost in tears when she told me about Plymouth. One has an idea that they must become bored by endless visits but I really believe that she cares very deeply.

I spoke to the Duke about France and Dunkirk. He was full of the right questions.

Chapter Forty-Seven

I was very pleased with the way the lunch went. Willy Teeling, who is very good at that sort of thing, arranged the lunch.

The Duke and Duchess drove to Belfast afterwards and I heard in the evening that the effect of their arrival was good. They bring some sort of influence with them. I don't know what it is, but people seemed to be reconciled after seeing them.

48

John had lost most of his possessions during the first year and a half of the war. Pilots learn to do with very little. They become casual about their clothes, their tennis racquets and their papers. The spaciousness of the life they live in the air seems to make them impatient with the little inanimate things most of us accumulate. John had flown from place to place over the face of Britain and he had shed most of his clothes and possessions on the way. But there was a black leather box to which he had clung all through the hazards of the war. It contained a jumble of papers, many of them notes or half-finished letters which he had written after some event or other.

But they are a jumble. He lived quickly and he had no time for the virtue of tidiness.

John's vice of not dating his letters and notes persisted. One of the papers in the box is an incomplete letter in which he described an evening at Aldergrove, when Phyllis Monkman arrived with her New Co-optimists to entertain the station. He wrote:

Phyllis Monkman has been here with a bunch of pretty girls and we all lost our hearts to them. What nice people! They go to the most outlandish places, in buses, miles and miles. Phyllis M told me that she can go on and on – the long journeys and the discomfort – because the troops make such a wonderful audience. They arrived in the late afternoon and the best we could do in the way of a theatre was the dining hall, with a hastily erected stage and RAF blue curtains which worked three times out of ten. We added some flags, some coloured paper and the station dance band. We arranged a special dressing room for her at the back of the stage, in what is normally the kitchen. She even had a tin basin in a stand and a jug of water. They took it all like lambs.

She is so willing to be kind to everybody. She was dazzling one minute, dancing, and then, almost before the curtains had closed and opened, she appeared again as a charwoman. She is a great trouper.

Afterwards, she came on and made us sing nice old songs like 'Turn the Dark Clouds Inside Out', 'Pack up Your Troubles', and, at the end, 'Abide With Me'.

I cannot tell you how touching it was, in that smoky room, after we had laughed and stamped and clapped ourselves silly, simply singing that calm and lovely hymn. The airmen loved it.

We went to the mess afterwards to give the cast some supper. Brian Hawkins (afterwards a prisoner of war in Occupied France), Denys Gathercole (still with the squadron), Peter Herrick (killed after John left the squadron), and Chipper chose their blondes and flirted violently. It was great fun. They took the girls back afterwards to Belfast in the squadron car. How they packed in I do not know. Phyllis Monkman and I leapt on to a table and did a tap dance. That was a moment! The Coastal Command squadron and my boys were delighted. I suppose they think me a bit pompous and quiet. They have never seen that side of me before. They didn't even know I could tap dance. It was a riot. They shrieked with delight when I kissed Phyllis Monkman after the tap dancing. She said that she wanted to give me something to keep my luck in. She looked at her rings and her watch and her pearls and said they meant nothing. She wanted to give me something that really meant something to her.

She suddenly put her hands behind her head and produced a long hair curler. She twisted it around my finger like a ring and said, 'There. You can't buy them now and that is the last one I have got.'

The boys all congratulated me next morning so I just thought I'd show them. They bet me a pound between them that I could not do a somersault in the air. I did it, in front of the mess.

A few days afterwards, John told me, the New Co-optimists were at Omagh, fifty or sixty miles away. The boys wanted to see their blondes again so he took them in the car. They drove like mad and arrived in time to have tea with them … eggs and bacon, toast and jam. Phyllis Monkman was there again. John wrote at the end of his note, 'She is a thoroughly nice person. She could not have been kinder to us. I admire her like hell. We all left with our pockets full of addresses.'

49

Death followed quickly on the days of fun. John wrote to me at the beginning of May:

What hell this is. Two of my boys were killed yesterday. I had sent them off to do air firing practice over Loch Neagh. It is just a normal affair and I did not think any more about it. Late in the afternoon Chipper said he wondered what had happened to them. They were fifteen minutes late. I had just come back after flying over to Loch Erne.

I did not worry about the boys at first. I thought that they were just being young and probably flying around and enjoying themselves. Then I realised so much time had passed that they could no longer have any petrol.

A watchman in a boat on the Loch had landed and telephoned to say that he thought he saw an aircraft crash into the water about twenty minutes before. Someone else who lived near the Loch rang up and said they had just been told that two aeroplanes had fallen into the water.

We have to be very careful because the Irish ring up with the most astonishing stories. But these horrible reports meant one thing to me. They had obviously collided.

Chipper and I ran to our aircraft and flew over the Loch. It was late and the light was fading. We searched the surface of the water. I found one patch of oil and Chipper found the other. There were little pieces of floating wreckage. It was quite horrible. I have never overcome my horror at losing youngsters when they are not in a battle. It seems so wasteful ... so wasteful after their training.

Chipper told me over the R/T that he had found the patch of oil and that he could see some fishermen lifting a body into a boat. I could see nothing but the oil patch.

I feel, more and more, that the bloodiness of it all is in peaceful accidents like this. They are shy to say so, but if these boys must die they wish to die in a battle. The speed of their life ... I cannot give you the word. But the speed of their life is such that they deserve to die in a combat. It is a pretty poor show when they just collide and crash into the water like that.

Pilley was so kind when I went back to the mess. I felt pretty shaken. Pilley is a Jew and they seem to understand. He came over to me and said, 'I am sorry. I realise so much what it must mean to you.' I went to bed early, feeling absolutely miserable.

50

On 10 May 1941, the *London Gazette* announced that John had been awarded a bar to his DFC because he had 'displayed great skill and initiative both as a squadron commander and as an individual fighter.' The notice added, 'he has destroyed twelve enemy aircraft of which two have been shot down at night.'

John amplified the news in a note which he wrote some days later:

I received the telegram while I was sitting in my office. I read it and threw it across to the Adj, who said, 'Congratulations, sir, may I go and tell the boys?' They soon came and leaned through the window, saying nice things. Chipper said, 'We presume that this means a party.' Well, it certainly did. When I went over to the mess in the evening there was a notice on the board from the PMC, to say that the Station Commander had approved of a party being given in my honour. Cocktails, supper and dancing. My squadron were to be the guests of the other members of the mess and everyone was allowed to bring a guest.

It was a riot. Hundreds of people Came to the cocktail party and the band played on the lawn. The Prime Minister of Northern Ireland came, and the Air Officer Commanding, Air Commodore Carr. Lord Londonderry was there also and he was most kind. He asked me if he could fly one of my Hurricanes. I do like him. He wants to, and could pilot anything. He is now sixty-three years old and he lives for flying.

The Station Commander made a speech and I was very touched. I think I told you before that we are lodgers here. The whole affair was a delightful gesture to the squadron. It is funny how one always feels such a fool. I felt terrible. I just spluttered, 'Thank you all very much.' I couldn't get what was in my heart out of my mouth.

The Station Commander and the Big White Chiefs left early and told us to get on with the party. And we did. We danced with the local lovelies, and when they left we sang songs and hovered about the buffet.

Tom Morgan has also got a bar to his, in the same *Gazette* as myself. We both have twelve Huns now. A couple of dozen between us. Good old 43.

51

On 14 May, John wrote:

I hope you received my wire. The whole affair was pure luck. It simply was a chance in a million. Yesterday morning I discovered that three of our aircraft were unserviceable. We had no spare tail-wheel tyres. I was angry. The spares had been used up and I had not been told. I rang up Killy who is now commanding a squadron at 'X.' He had some spares so I said I would fly over and take lunch from him and also collect the tyres. It was good hearing his voice.

The weather was pretty bloody but I took off at 11.30 and set course over the Irish Sea. I flew into thick fog which was down to sea level. I could see nothing and, as one day would make no difference, I turned back.

During the afternoon the weather improved and the fog lifted over the Irish Sea. It suddenly became a perfect spring evening with broken cloud at 3,000 feet and a blue sky above. I decided to have another shot at it, so I took off about 5 o'clock. The morning fog had gone and the Irish Sea was calm and smooth. Not a white horse in sight. The sun was so strong that I could see my own shadow moving over the water. I was flying quite low. It was so clear that I could see the coast of Scotland while I was still flying over the Irish coast.

As you know, we have had a few sneak raiders in these parts. They fly up the Irish Channel, just above the water, to avoid detection. They have done a certain amount of damage to shipping … but nothing to write home about. I have always made it a rule for myself and my boys to cross the Channel low, just in case we might meet one of them. But it has never happened.

I was halfway across when I saw an aircraft flying north at sea level. He was about two miles away and I just hoped that it would be a Hun. But I suspected that it was only an Anson or something on a training exercise. I made a savage dart towards it and as I approached I realised that it was going too quickly for an Anson. Nearer, and I could recognise its dirty green paint and a faint swastika on the tail. It was a Dornier 17. He was between me and the Scottish coast, heading towards Glasgow. I had never attacked a Hun as near the water before. He was no more than twenty feet above the surface. I could not get at him from underneath or from dead astern without running the risk of getting into his slipstream and going into the drink myself. However, I dived on him and fired. His top gunner had started firing as I dived, but apparently my first shot got him as I heard no more from him. But the burst didn't seem to have done much else although I knew that I had hit his wings with my incendiaries. I had seen them striking. I turned away and came in again to attack. As I turned I saw that my first burst had done more than I thought. Blue-grey smoke was pouring from the starboard engine. I fired at the engine again and it stopped. The Hun tooled along slowly and turned towards the Scottish coast. I opened my throttle, got in front of him and made a desperate head-on attack, firing my final squirt when close on his beam. My last bullet seemed to finish him. I was flying at about 100 feet and he was scratching the waves below me. I have never been so close to the actual destruction of my enemy in daylight before ... as I was when the Dornier hit the sea. He turned over on his back so that the pale blue under-surface of his aircraft showed as it sank slowly, nose first, in the still water. There was a patch of burning oil and I circled round to watch the Dornier slowly sinking beneath it, the Hun crosses shivering in the water.

There was no sign of anybody trying to get out. I suppose they had been killed by the impact. I pressed the tit of the R/T to tell my story to the Controller. They were highly delighted and as surprised as I was. There was still plenty of time so I waited until there was only the patch of burning oil. Then I flew on and found a little ship near the coast of Scotland. I circled over it and then headed off to guide them to the patch of burning oil, in case anything appeared. They followed, so I left them and flew off to collect the tyres. I felt a bit shy as I had shot down the Hun outside my territory, actually in Killy's. I was a poacher. Loel Guinness, whose squadrons were after the same Hun, sent me a telegram which reached me soon after I got back. He said, 'Strongly object to you throwing your dirt on our doorstep. Congratulations all the same.'

I did not see anyone when I landed. The tyres were waiting for me and Killy was away. They tied the tyres into the fuselage and I started for home.

I flew home high, feeling rather elated. I had not even bothered to have my guns re-armed. It is the first daylight victory for my squadron since they came to Northern Ireland. This one pleased me because it was rather difficult. He was bloody near the water and he nearly foxed me.

I felt a bit embarrassed when I arrived back and the boys were waiting for me. It honestly seems unfair that I should have all the luck. It would do them so much good if they could see a Hun or two. I really felt almost ashamed when I saw Chipper and Brian. They spend hours at readiness and they escort convoy after convoy. But there is never a Hun about for them to have a crack at.

We all went into Belfast for a party afterwards. But I felt an odd depression before I went. I got rid of it by having a bath. I felt as if I smelled of Hun. Well, that's my thirteenth. And it was shot down on the 13th. Is that a bad omen?

52

The tiredness that comes to seasoned pilots is not easy to explain. It seems that they live so violently during their combats that they squeeze ten years of experience into the space of two. The result of two or three years of operational flying is that they need long periods of sleep while they are on the ground because they pour unnatural forces and strength into their combats in the air. It is not strange for a pilot who has landed after a battle to fall upon his bed and sleep the clock round.

I write of those who have survived numerous battles over a period of years. They are veterans while they are still in their twenties. Also, they have assumed the duties of squadron leaders or wing commanders, with the responsibility of other lives in their hands.

A little time before Paddy Finucane was killed I was sent to do a job on his station. I remember walking along a passage in the mess and seeing his name on the door of his bedroom, *Wing Commander Finucane, DSO, DFC.* At that moment he was leading a wing of three squadrons in a fighter sweep over occupied territory. He was twenty-one and he had little knowledge of the world. Yet he had brought down twenty-eight enemy aircraft, and he was obliged to know enough of human nature to inspire confidence in the thirty-six pilots who followed him ... a fantastic burden for a boy who might still have been swinging a tennis racquet on the banks of the Liffey. I met him afterwards and we walked across the aerodrome. He was easy to talk to ... bewildered by his fame and concerned lest it should interfere with his duty to the Service. It seemed incredible to me that one so young could have gathered so much history about him. His combats were only part of his story. The real value of his work lay in the command he had over those who flew with him and believed in him.

The emotional and mental attitude towards the war seems to change in these pilots who grow old so quickly. Three years or so ago they were crying, 'Please God send us a nice war!' It was the natural cry of boys who had been trained to fly and to fight. There was a certain thoughtless gallantry in their prayer. But this seems to have changed with experience. Their intentions have become more grim. Now they have an account to settle with the enemy because they realise the fullness of his infamy and because they have their dead friends to avenge. The mature pilots in the Service are out to kill, without any songs upon their lips or muddling of conscience.

I once heard Denys Gillam, who has a DSO, a DFC with bar, and an AFC, say to an American who asked him what he felt about shooting down Huns, 'I am a professional soldier and my job is to kill.' His voice was fierce with determination. Three years ago he might have said, 'Oh, I just like having a crack at the wicked enemy.'

These pilots have suffered and they have grown wise. Flying is no longer merely a personal excitement to them. It has become more passionate than that. They may have their gay moments on leave, but for most of the time, all their valuable forces are poured into battle. While they are not flying, they sleep and rest and discipline their bodies, as part of their dedication to the war. Now they are concerned over the future of the world and they speak of this as part of their object in fighting.

These changes had come to John as they had come to almost every other pilot who survived the first two years of the war. He had been a little sentimental about killing enemy pilots when the war began. I always suspected that he felt the death of his first victim more than he admitted. There is a bond between pilots, whatever their nationality, and at the beginning of the war this bond had to be broken down. John used to insist on his respect for the German pilot as a fighter. But practice developed the will and ruthlessness of a soldier in him. He soon came to know that it was through the destruction of those pilots and their aircraft that he could hit at the heart of Nazi Germany.

But the two years had made him very tired. When he was on leave he would sleep for stretches of twelve and fourteen hours and wake up to find that he had torn his bed clothes while he slept. Perhaps old combats were fought again in the darkness of the night. I protested after one such experience and said, 'You should rest now. You have done your bit.'

His answer was angry. 'That is a weak thing to say. I admit that I am tired. But I have no thought except to win the war. I am going to be useful for as long as I can. That is my faith. I won't admit that I am tired to anybody in the Service. If I did, I would be ashamed of myself for as long as I lived.'

But he could not hide his exhaustion from those in command. At the end of June he was posted from his squadron to the comparative rest of a staff job with one of the Groups.

He wrote:

They say that I am to be posted to a desk to do a staff job. I am now classed as a tired pilot and I am miserable beyond words. The thought of having to hand over all that I have built up and loved here makes me very sad. But I am tired so I suppose they are right.

William Teeling, who was also stationed at John's station, wrote a fuller story of his farewell in a letter:

He came here to do a difficult job; to a squadron which was browned off at being left so long out of action and because they had lost all their best pilots, one by one, to reinforce other squadrons. The way John made himself their leader and in every sense their confidant was a remarkable feat. I know of few others who could have done it. John has made his squadron popular and himself above all.

The coastal boys have shown how sorry they are that he is going and so have many others. The Londonderrys at Mount Stewart are really sorry to see him go. He liked going over there and wandering about the garden. Lord Londonderry told me that he thought John was one of the nicest and least assuming squadron commanders he had met. And he ought to know because Lord L lives for the RAF in Northern Ireland.

A few days ago three of us decided to motor John to Newcastle, in the Mountains of Mourne, to give him a farewell twenty-four hours. We got as far as Lady Clanwilliam's at Ballynahinch for lunch. Her daughter, Biddy Herman, and one or two others said that they did not see why they should not join us, so they got the local billeting major to lend his car. We drove to Newcastle and when we arrived we were joined by Mike Sayers, the Irish rugger international, and some of his regiment. They asked if they could come, because John had always been so helpful with the army when they wanted to see what the Air Force was doing. They in turn brought along the Kilmorey girls from Mourne Park, with a party. Gerry Annesley, not to be outdone, got over some bottles of wine from his place nearby and when we got to the Slieve Donard hotel our party of three had grown into a party of about forty.

John's squadron was very busy and no more could be spared during the day to come with us. But three of the pilots motored all the sixty miles when they finished their work to dine with him. They had to go back the same sixty miles afterwards in the blackout. It only shows how fond they are of him.

On Sunday, as lovely a day as Ireland can produce, we went on to Mourne Park where the Kilmoreys gave us lunch. 'K,' always the perfect host, was particularly keen to meet John as he actually saw him shoot down the first Hun over Northern Ireland and saw the Heinkel disappear into the sea.

It is a bit sad seeing him now that we are back at Aldergrove, handing over. It will be difficult to imagine a certain radiator in the mess, in a certain corner of the hall before lunch, before dinner and before bed, without John standing there, holding a can of beer, with four or five of his pilots around him. There is a brass bucket about ten feet away and they have become expert shots at throwing their cigarette ends into it. If the pilot leaning against the radiator misses the bucket he has to go and pick the cigarette end up and resign his place at the radiator to the next man. They made the time pass as only contented and interested people can. I shall feel damned lonely without him and I won't be the only one.

John closed this part of his story with a letter written on 12 June:

I feel like hell. My story with the squadron comes to an end. The boys arranged a dinner for me the night before last at Hall's Hotel in Antrim. They all went ahead of me and told me that I had to wait downstairs until I was sent for. I drank some cocktails and then Chipper came down for me. He took me up to the dance hall. They had been working on it, red roses on the table and paper rose petals put all around my chair, a great armchair in which I had to be propped up with cushions. Each place had a name card in front of it and a bottle of each person's favourite drink. A glass of milk for Chipper because he never touches alcohol. In front of me was a small parcel, but I was not allowed to open it until midnight.

We had lovely fun. Hanging from the centre of the danceroom was one of those revolving chandeliers that send spotlights on the dancers. Chipper had found the picture of a naked baby, lying on a rug. Under it they had painted, *John as a child*. They had hung it on the revolving light so that it went round and round all through dinner. I persuaded Chipper to have a drink and he got quite tight, for the first time in his life. We sang all the old songs and played rough games. Then we danced the Palais Glide. This was a staggering performance. We made speeches and said nice things about each other.

There were three American pilots who have not been with us very long. It was their first sight of the Royal Air Force at play and they loved it. I think they thought the English were a lot of sour pusses before they came over here. But now they are convinced that we are human. The Poles came too. I wish you could have seen the Americans and the Poles doing the Palais Glide. Afterwards we slid up and down the polished floor on cushions.

Then somebody came in and said the Sergeant Pilots were waiting in the bar to buy me a drink. So I joined them. The Czechs came too. I feel it very much leaving them because I honestly feel that I have helped them to understand us.

Just before I left, I undid the parcel. It was a gold penknife with my name on it and a note that said 'To John with love from his boys.'

I leave tomorrow and I am busy handing over to Francis Blackadder who is taking my place. He is a brilliant rugger player with a first-class brain. He is a strict disciplinarian and his methods will be different from mine. But I like him and I think he will do well.

Three days later John wrote from Scotland:

> Well, it is all over. I am on my way to that bloody desk. I came over in a Hudson and my old squadron with twelve aircraft, escorted me across the channel and circled overhead while I landed. Chipper was on one side with a flight of three and Brian Hawkins on the other. I prayed for a Hun to appear. I couldn't have done anything about it in the Hudson but they would have given it bloody hell.

53

John's long letters and combat reports came to an end. There were occasional notes and telephone calls from his desk. 'This bloody green-topped desk is wearing me out,' he wrote. 'It is stained with the ink spots of all the other stooges who have sat at it before me.'

Early in June he wrote, 'There is one bright spot in this weary life. The Czechs have given me a decoration. Yesterday morning a letter arrived from Air Vice-Marshal Janoušek to say that I had been awarded the Czechoslovak Air Force Pilot's badge as a mark of gratitude and appreciation for my help to the Czech pilots. The decoration is an enormous badge which I wear over my right-hand pocket. I am beginning to look like Goering.'

Then came a note, 'I am still very tired and I feel ill. But I am scared of going to the MO in case he posts me sick and then I'd lose my new job. I am coming up to see the Monarch to get my bar on 6 July. Could you arrange for a doctor to see me the evening before? I am in such pain all the time and I don't want to pass out at the feet of the King.'

There was a doctor waiting when John arrived in London. The verdict was simple and rather frightening. There was an abscess in his lower bowel, within twenty-four hours of bursting, and the doctor insisted on an immediate operation. John agreed to go into a nursing home when the Investiture was over.

On fine days, the King stands in the courtyard of Buckingham Palace to decorate the sailors, the soldiers and pilots. 6 July was a coldish day and the ceremony was in the entrance hall where the walls awaken scenes of 100 years ago, with early Winterhalter portraits of the old Duchess of Kent, the young Queen and her husband.

A band played some gay tunes but otherwise, there was no sign that this was a special day. The King walked on to a low dais and pinned the medals on the heroes, one after the other, in the long procession. There was not a glimmer of pomp. One felt that he had simply asked them into his house to thank them for what they had done.

Mothers, wives and sisters had come to look on; old mothers in spick and span black dresses, with faces and hands that told the story of work. Young wives with children. Fathers from the countryside in gleaming white collars and Sunday suits. It was a domestic and unpretentious scene rather than a ceremony. A year before when he appeared before the King to receive his DFC, John's arm had been in a sling. The royal memory did not fail. The King asked him, 'How many have you destroyed?'

John replied, 'Thirteen, sir.'

Then the King asked, 'When did you get your DFC?'

John told him that it was in June of the previous year.

The King asked, 'Wasn't your arm in a sling?'

John walked out of the Palace, beneath the balcony from

which Queen Victoria waved farewell to the soldiers leaving for the Crimea. It seemed that he was taking his place in an old and splendid company.

That afternoon John went into the nursing home. About four days afterwards a nurse walked into his bedroom and said, 'There's a telephone message just come for you. Somebody has told the King that you are ill and he has sent a message to say that he hopes you will soon be better.'

List of Illustrations

1. Peter Townsend and Caesar Hull. Caesar shot down four German aircraft on one mission in Norway in an antiquated Gladiator biplane. © The Alfred & Isabel & Marian Reed Trust.

2. Laurie Lorimer and George Feeny. © The Alfred & Isabel & Marian Reed Trust.

3. Members of 43 Squadron photographed in the North of Scotland. Left to right: Sergeant Buck, Pilot Officer Tony Woods-Scawen who was shot down and saved by the same parachute six times. Asked why he carried his parachute 20 miles across France he'd said 'well, I know this one works'. Flight Lieutenant Caesar Hull, Flying Officer Wilkinson, Sergeant Garton. © The Alfred & Isabel & Marian Reed Trust.

4. Larch trees cut down by John Simpson's aircraft when it crashed on 21 February 1940. © The Alfred & Isabel & Marian Reed Trust.

5. Fitters and riggers carrying out an inspection on John Simpson's Hurricane. © The Alfred & Isabel & Marian Reed Trust.

6. Armourers re-arming John Simpson's Hurricane. © The Alfred & Isabel & Marian Reed Trust.

7. John Simpson briefing pilots of his squadron in Northern Ireland. © The Alfred & Isabel & Marian Reed Trust.

8. Dickie Lee. © The Alfred & Isabel & Marian Reed Trust.

9. Kitson with two friends, before he joined his squadron. © The Alfred & Isabel & Marian Reed Trust.

10. George Lott. © The Alfred & Isabel & Marian Reed Trust.

11. 43 Squadron. John Simpson is fourth from the left. © Jonathan Reeve.

12. Blenheims over south east England, 1940. John's squadron had a 'pool' Blenheim which he flew to Blackpool for a few days leave with MacEwen on 3 February 1940. © Jonathan Reeve JR1626b82p64 19391945.

13. Readiness. © The Alfred & Isabel & Marian Reed Trust.

14. Ground crew rearming Hurricanes. From the Battle of Britain Monument (Victoria embankment, London) sculptured by Paul Day. Photo © Jonathan Reeve.

15. Ground staff overhauling the Rolls Royce Merlin engine in the Hurricane. © Jonathan Reeve JR1233b71pic13 19391945.

16. Hurricanes being refuelled immediately on return to their base. © Jonathan Reeve JR1234b71pic14 19391945.

17. Women at work in fighter aircraft production. From the Battle of Britain Monument (Victoria embankment, London) sculptured by Paul Day. Photo © Jonathan Reeve.

18. An aircraft spotter of the Observer Corps on the roof of a building in London on the look out for enemy aircraft, 1940. St Paul's Cathedral is in the background. © Jonathan Reeve.

19. Observer Corps on the look out for enemy aircraft. After radar they were the second line of defense. From the Battle of Britain Monument (Victoria embankment, London) sculptured by Paul Day. Photo © Jonathan Reeve.

20. Operations Room. It was from here that John Simpson would be directed towards enemy aircraft via his R/T. © Jonathan Reeve JR1214b69pic15 19391945.

21. An air battle is in progress. In the Operations Room of a fighter station Plotters with their croupier-like sticks mark up the position of the aircraft, while others man operational telephones. © Jonathan Reeve JR1333b69pic49 19391945.

22. A plotter takes tally cards to mark up the position of squadrons on the indicator board. © Jonathan Reeve JR1335b69pic48 19391945.

23. In the Control Room of a fighter station R/T operators keep contact with pilots. One operator marks up the position of a fighter on the indicator board, while others give pilots instructions to land. © Jonathan Reeve JR1359b69pic74 19391945.

24. A view of the operations room showing plotters at work on the table, a wartime image issued to the press with the actual plotting map obliterated for security reasons. © Jonathan Reeve JR1352b69pic66 19391945. ?38.

25. Three fighter pilots live in a caravan beside their aircraft ready for instant action. © Jonathan Reeve JR1235b71pic15 19391945.

26. Fighter pilots pass the time waiting for action 1940. © Jonathan Reeve JR1236b71pic16 19391945.

27. A typical scene in a dispersal hut showing members of a fighter squadron waiting for the call for action, 1940. © Jonathan Reeve JR1622b82p60-1 19391945.

28. Fighter pilots play ha'penny while they wait for the call to 'scramble', 1940. © Jonathan Reeve JR1623b82p62 19391945.

29. 'Scramble'. From the alert relayed from a fighter station to the airfields fighters could be in the air within minutes. From the Battle of Britain Monument (Victoria embankment, London) sculptured by Paul Day. Photo © Jonathan Reeve.

30. Pilots scramble to their Spitfires, June 1940. © Jonathan Reeve JR1631b83p234T 19391945

31. A fighter pilot springs into action when the order comes, 1940. © Jonathan Reeve JR1625b82p63B 19391945.

32. A Hawker Hurricane 8-gun fighter as flown by John Simpson. © Jonathan Reeve JR1208b71pic3 19391945.

33. Formations of Hurricanes, 1940. John Simpson didn't take to flying in formation very quickly. 1940. © Jonathan Reeve JR1448b79p3T 19391945.

34. Spitfire returning from a combat mission, August 1940. John Simpson tried the Spitfire but preferred Hurricanes. © Jonathan Reeve JR1226b71pic4 19391945.

35. Spitfire in flight, 1940. © Jonathan Reeve JR1228b71pic6 19391945.

36. Spitfires on patrol, 1940. © Jonathan Reeve JR1624b82p62-3T 19391945.

37. Hurricanes pulling away after making contact with German aircraft. © Jonathan Reeve JR1209b71pic9 19391945.

38. Formations of Hurricanes, 1940. © Jonathan Reeve JR1554b79p25 19391945.

39. A Ju 87 'Skuka' dive bomber. © Tom Neil.

40. An Me 110. © Tom Neil.

41. An Me 109 in flight. © Jonathan Reeve JR1445b78me109p 19391945.

42. A Dornier 17. From the Battle of Britain Monument (Victoria embankment, London) sculptured by Paul Day. Photo © Jonathan Reeve.

43. A Ju 88. © Jonathan Reeve JR1446b78pju88 19391945.

44. A Hurricane attacking an Me 109. From the Battle of Britain Monument (Victoria embankment, London) sculptured by Paul Day. Photo © Jonathan Reeve.

45. & 46. Air combat, a Spitfire pilot trying to avoid cannon shells fired from an ME 109 on his tail. From the Battle of Britain Monument (Victoria embankment, London) sculptured by Paul Day. Photo © Jonathan Reeve.

47. A fighter pilot with R/T equipment. From the Battle of Britain Monument (Victoria embankment, London) sculptured by Paul Day. Photo © Jonathan Reeve.

48. Air combat, a Spitfire pilot trying to avoid cannon shells fired from an ME 109 on his tail. From the Battle of Britain Monument (Victoria embankment, London) sculptured by Paul Day. Photo © Jonathan Reeve.

49, 50. & 51. British gun-camera images of German aircraft being shot down. © Jonathan Reeve JR1215b69pic70 19391945, © Jonathan Reeve JR1451b79p33 19391945, © Jonathan Reeve JR1452b79p32 19391945.

52. The Battle of Britain was very visible to the British from the ground with swirling vapour trails marking the dogfights in the summer skies of 1940. © Jonathan Reeve JR1630b82p84T 19391945.

53. A doomed German Dornier 17 bomber aircraft plummeting earthwards after being attacked by British fighters. © Jonathan Reeve JR1449b79p31 19391945.

54. A downed Me 109. This was the Luftwaffe's main fighter. © Jonathan Reeve JR1211b71pic18 19391945.

55. A downed He 111. © Jonathan Reeve JR1212b71pic20 19391945.

56. A downed Dornier 17, August 1940. © Jonathan Reeve JR1600b83p299B 19391945.

57. A Dornier 17 after having crash-landed, 1940. © Jonathan Reeve JR1450b79p35B 19391945.

58. An RAF pilot bailing out. © Jonathan Reeve JR1213b71pic83 19391945.

59. 'Down in the drink'. A pilot who bailed out over the Channel is rescued by an air/sea rescue launch. © Jonathan Reeve JR1356b69pic71 19391945.

60. A Hurricane coming in to refuel and re-arm. A photograph taken during the Battle of Britain. © Jonathan Reeve JR1210b71pic12 19391945.

61. A Hurricane fighter pilot having returned from a combat mission, 1940 . © Jonathan Reeve JR1242b71pic26 19391945.

62. A fighter pilot in full flying gear on the wing of his Hurricane. © Jonathan Reeve JR1239b71pic22 19391945.

63. On return to base pilots would be debriefed by the squadron intelligence officer who would complete a 'combat report' including details on any 'kills'. © Tom Neil.

64. John Simpson's combat report (from which the original 1943 edition of this book took its name) for his shooting down of his thirteenth 'kill' a Dornier 17. With thanks to Robert Walsh.

65. Nurses look after wounded RAF officers on the terrace of a hospital. Battle of Britain veteran Tom Neil: 'Our killing fields were roughly over the central part of Kent. Everyone in the squadron was shot down at one time or another. We got to know the hospitals in Kent like the backs of our hands'. © Jonathan Reeve JR1629b82p230-1 19391945.

66. The Dornier 17 'Flying Pencil', the most frequently encountered German bomber during the Battle of Britain. From the Battle of Britain Monument (Victoria embankment, London) sculptured by Paul Day. Photo © Jonathan Reeve.

67. Anti-aircraft gunners firing on German raiders above. From the Battle of Britain Monument (Victoria embankment, London) sculptured by Paul Day. Photo © Jonathan Reeve.

68. The Dornier 17 'Flying Pencil', the most frequently encountered German bomber during the Battle of Britain. From the Battle of Britain Monument (Victoria embankment, London) sculptured by Paul Day. Photo © Jonathan Reeve.

69. St Pauls through the smoke of the great fire raid of Sunday 29 December 1940. © Jonathan Reeve.

70. Firemen of the London Auxiliary Fire Fighting Services during the Blitz, 1940. © Jonathan Reeve.

71, 72. & 73. John Simpson and his fellow pilots were very conscious of the human cost of the blitz. © Jonathan Reeve. © Jonathan Reeve JR1627b82p102 19391945.

74. Winston Churchill surveys the Blitz-damaged House of Commons. © Jonathan Reeve JR1628b82p126 19391945.

75. A classic photograph of Hurricane pilots taken at the height of the Battle of Britain in July 1940. © Jonathan Reeve JR1453b79p2&3 19391945.

76. One of the iconic images created by the Air Ministry of a Battle of Britain fighter pilot. © Jonathan Reeve JR1240b71pic23 19391945.

77. Cover of the 1941 Ministry of Information propaganda booklet which was the first book to lionise the 'Few'. It sold in the 100,000s. © Jonathan Reeve.

78. 43 Squadron emblem. From the Battle of Britain Monument (Victoria embankment, London) sculptured by Paul Day. Photo © Jonathan Reeve.

79. John W. C. Simpson's name on the Battle of Britain monument on Victoria embankment in London. Photo © Jonathan Reeve.

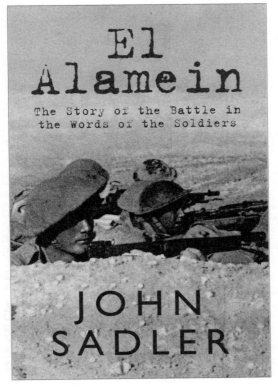

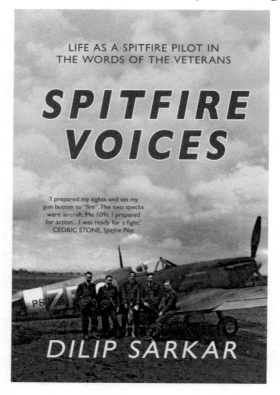

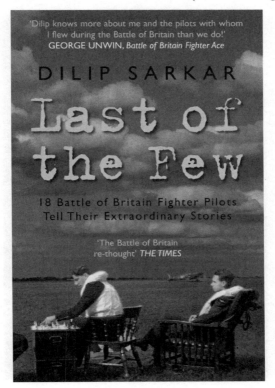

Also available from Amberley Publishing

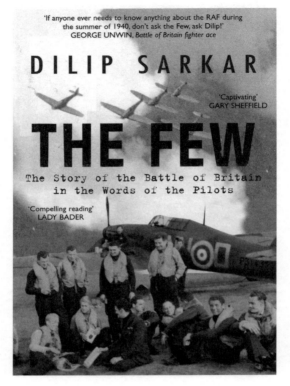

'If anyone ever needs to know anything about the RAF during the summer of 1940, don't ask the Few, ask Dilip!'
GEORGE UNWIN, *Battle of Britain fighter ace*

DILIP SARKAR

'Captivating'
GARY SHEFFIELD

THE FEW

The Story of the Battle of Britain in the Words of the Pilots

'Compelling reading'
LADY BADER

The history of the Battle of Britain in the words of the pilots

'Over the last 30 years Dilip Sarkar has sought out and interviewed or corresponded with numerous survivors worldwide. Many of these were not famous combatants, but those who formed the unsung backbone of Fighter Command in 1940. Without Dilip's patient recording and collation of their memories, these survivors would not have left behind a permanent record.' LADY BADER
'A well-researched detailed chronicle of the Battle of Britain'. HUGH SEBAG MONTEFIORE

£9.99 Paperback
129 photographs
320 pages
978-1-4456-0701-6

Also available as an ebook
Available from all good bookshops or to order direct
Please call **01453-847-800**
www.amberleybooks.com

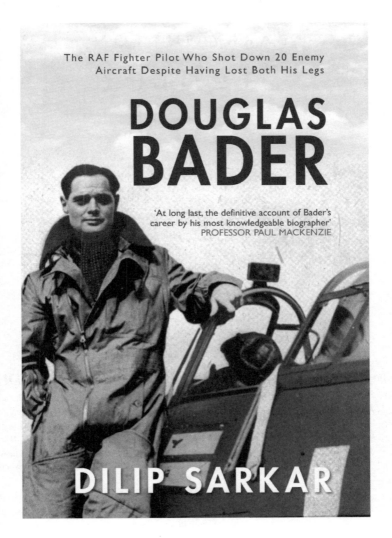

Also available from Amberley Publishing

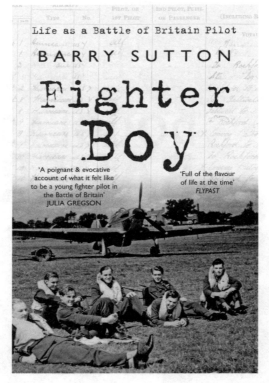

The Battle of Britain memoir of Hurricane pilot Barry Sutton, DFC

'A refreshing book written just after the events' *INTERCOM: THE AIRCREW ASSOCIATION*

'The reader will find in Squadron Leader Sutton the virtues which the country has come to admire in the RAF flier – courage, determination, persistence, unfailing good humour, optimism, faith' *THE TIMES*

At 23 years of age, Barry Sutton had experienced more than the average person experiences in a lifetime. This book, based on a diary he kept during the war, covers September 1939 to September 1940 when he was shot down and badly burned.

£10.99 Paperback
61 illustrations
192 pages
978-1-4456-0627-9

Also available as an ebook
Available from all good bookshops or to order direct
Please call **01453–847–800**
www.amberleybooks.com

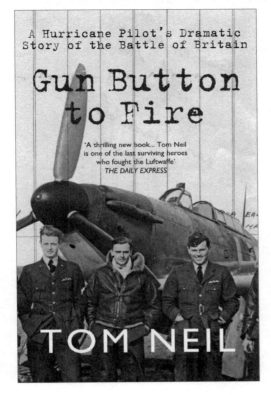

Also available from Amberley Publishing

How to fly the legendary fighter plane in combat using the manuals and instructions supplied by the RAF during the Second World War

'A Must' *INTERCOM: THE AIRCREW ASSOCIATION*

An amazing array of leaflets, books and manuals were issued by the War Office during the Second World War to aid pilots in flying the Supermarine Spitfire, here for the first time they are collated into a single book with the original 1940s setting. An introduction is supplied by expert aviation historian Dilip Sarkar. Other sections include aircraft recognition, how to act as an RAF officer, bailing out etc.

£9.99 Paperback
40 illustrations
264 pages
978-1-84868-436-2

Also available as an ebook
Available from all good bookshops or to order direct
Please call **01453-847-800**
www.amberleybooks.com

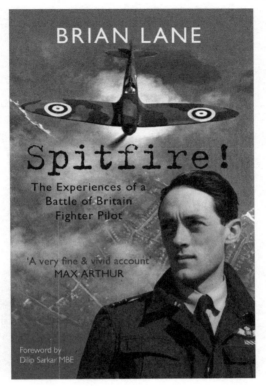

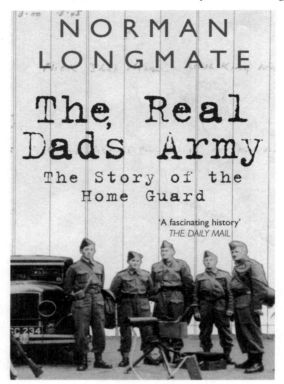